THE BREADMACHINE BIBLE

THE BREADMACHINE BIBLE

MORE THAN 100 RECIPES FOR
DELICIOUS HOME BAKING
WITH YOUR BREADMACHINE

ANNE SHEASBY

dbp

DUNCAN BAIRD PUBLISHERS

LONDON

THE BREADMACHINE BIBLE
Anne Sheasby

First published in the United Kingdom and Ireland in
2009 by Duncan Baird Publishers Ltd
Sixth Floor, Castle House
75–76 Wells Street
London W1T 3QH

This paperback edition first published in 2011

Conceived, created and designed by Duncan Baird
Publishers Ltd

British Library Cataloguing-in-Publication Data:
A CIP record for this book is available from the
British Library

Managing Editor: Sarah Epton
Managing Designer: Manisha Patel
Designer: Saliesh Patel
Commissioned Photography: William Lingwood
Food Stylist: Bridget Sargeson
Prop Stylist: Helen Trent

ISBN: 978-1-84483-938-4

10 9 8 7 6 5 4 3 2 1

Typeset in DIN and Univers
Colour reproduction by Colourscan, Singapore
Printed in Singapore by Imago

Publisher's note: While every care has been taken
in compiling the recipes for this book, Duncan Baird
Publishers, or any other persons who have been
involved in working on this publication, cannot accept
responsibility for any errors or omissions, inadvertent
or not, that may be found in the recipes or text, nor for
any problems that may arise as a result of preparing
one of these recipes. If you are pregnant or breast-
feeding or have any special dietary requirements or
medical conditions, it is advisable to consult a medical
professional before following any of the recipes
contained in this book.

a note about the recipes

Please note that metric, imperial and cup measurements are
given for the recipes. Follow one set of measures only, not a
mixture, as they are not interchangeable.

All spoon and cup measures are level unless otherwise
stated. Sets of measuring spoons are available in metric and
imperial for accurate measurements. Liquid measures are as
follows:

    1 teaspoon (tsp) = 5ml
    1 tablespoon (tbsp) = 15ml
    1 cup = 250ml

Medium eggs should be used in the recipes, unless specified
otherwise.

We have included cooking temperatures for electric and
gas ovens. Remember if you have a fan-assisted oven that you
need to reduce the oven temperature slightly (usually by around
20 degrees) and/or adjust the cooking times. Please refer to
the manufacturer's guidelines for more specific information.

Please note that breadmachines vary, so add the
ingredients to the bread pan in the order specified in your
instruction manual (if this differs from the instructions given
in these recipes). The order in which we recommend that
you add the ingredients to your bread pan will be applicable
to many, but not all, breadmachines, so please ensure that
you read and follow your manufacturer's instruction book
carefully before preparing any of these recipes.

contents

bread over the centuries

Bread has been part of the staple diet of many countries worldwide for thousands of years and it is still held in high esteem within many cultures. Bread forms an important part of our everyday diet, providing a good, basic food that is both nutritious and delicious.

In centuries gone by, bread was initially baked over open fires, but gradually traditional ovens of brick or stone were built into homes or bakeries. Such ovens are still in use in the more rural areas of countries around the world, but the advance of technology and the development of modern ovens has seen the traditional types much less used. Over time, an increasing range of breads has been created, and new ingredients and flavourings have been discovered and added to basic recipes. Today we have a vast range of delicious loaves available to us in all shapes and sizes, offering many different tastes and textures.

Bakers, grocers, delicatessens, farmers' markets and supermarkets stock an array of traditional loaves as well as popular regional loaves and breads from around the world. We can choose from sweet or savoury breads, some plain, others flavoured with ingredients such as seeds, olives, cheese, herbs, sun-dried tomatoes, spices or fruit. An increasing range of organic and specialist breads, such as gluten-free or dairy-free breads, is also readily available, and craft bakers offer traditional loaves as well as creating new and interesting breads.

Nevertheless, it's hard to beat the rich aroma and full flavour of freshly made home-baked loaves, and making your own bread can be simple and very rewarding, especially with the use of a breadmachine. These increasingly popular appliances are ideal for those of us with little time to spare, providing the satisfaction of baking your own bread using fresh, nourishing ingredients.

our daily bread

Bread is an appetising food as well as being nutritious, and we should try to include a good proportion of starchy foods, such as bread, in our everyday diet. Many basic breads are low in fat, and bread provides an excellent source of starch – the more complex carbohydrate that provides the body with a sustained energy source – as well as some protein. All breads provide dietary fibre, and wholemeal and wholewheat varieties contain nearly four times more than white loaves, in addition to lots of B vitamins and some iron. White flour is generally fortified with calcium, so in fact, white bread can contribute significantly to calcium intake.

Obviously, some of the more elaborate enriched breads and doughs contain more calories and fat than basic loaves, but these too can be enjoyed as special-occasion breads or treats within a balanced diet. Many of the quick breads such as teabreads can also provide healthy snacks.

breadmachine recipes for all types of bread

This book by no means includes all breadmachine recipes, but it offers many different types of breads from all over the world, enabling you to create tasty breads in your own home at a fraction of the cost of commercially produced loaves.

We include the basics of breadmaking and breadmachines, essential information on key ingredients and techniques, as well as some useful hints and tips. Each recipe section is filled with a tempting selection of recipes, ranging from simple, rustic everyday breads to enriched, speciality loaves, and from traditional flat breads to quick and easy teabreads and tea-time treats. We also include a section on gluten-free breads, for those with a sensitivity to gluten.

Each recipe is clearly written and easy to follow, and includes guidance tips such as preparation and cooking times, as well as the number of servings.

By mastering your breadmachine, and using the recipes in this book as a guide, you can experiment with all kinds of flavours, shapes and textures to suit your own tastes. So we invite you to take a leisurely journey through this eclectic collection and hope that you will enjoy the experience of creating and baking your own bread at home for many months and years to come.

ingredients for breadmaking

Bread has four essential ingredients: flour, yeast, liquid and salt. Other ingredients such as sugar, fat and eggs may be added to produce different types of bread.

Flour

Types of flour

For traditional yeasted breads made in a breadmachine, choose strong wheat flour, also known as breadmaking flour or bread flour. It is available in several varieties, the most common being white, brown, wholemeal, granary and soft grain white. Strong or bread flour has a high gluten content, which stretches the dough and traps in air as it cooks, to give a well-shaped loaf with a good rise and a light, open texture. Flours vary between brands, but choose organic, unbleached strong flour, if possible.

Plain or self-raising flours are generally used only in yeast-free and quick breads (although some yeasted doughs, such as French Bread, use a mixture of flours). Quick breads tend to have a closer, more crumbly texture.

Breads made with strong wholemeal flour tend to be slightly denser and coarser in texture than white breads, but are flavourful and nutritious. For a lighter-textured loaf, you can use half strong white and half strong wholemeal flour. Strong brown flour will produce a lighter brown loaf, whereas strong granary or malthouse flour (which is a mixture of strong brown flour and malted wheat flakes or grains), gives a nutty, malted flavour. Strong granary flour may also be made from a combination of strong wholemeal and white flours, sometimes with rye flour added, and malted wheat grains. Stoneground flour (available in wholemeal and brown varieties) is ground between stones, hence the name, and this gives the flour a slightly roasted, nutty flavour. Strong soft grain flour is strong white flour with kibbled grains of wheat and rye added.

Other flours such as barley, millet and spelt flours have a low gluten content, but can be combined with strong bread flours to make delicious loaves. Rye flour, which has a good gluten content, often produces dough that is sticky and difficult to handle, so it is frequently mixed with other flours to make it more manageable.

Gluten-free flours

If you have an intolerance of or sensitivity to gluten, you will need to avoid flours that contain gluten. Because gluten is the protein that strengthens and binds dough in baking, you may need to find alternative binding agents when using gluten-free flours. A combination of starches often works better than a single type, and adding ingredients such as egg, grated apple or mashed banana may also help. It should be noted that gluten-free flours tend to make denser loaves with a closer texture, and also that they tend to absorb more liquid than ordinary flours, so you may need to add a little more liquid to all your dough mixtures if you are adapting standard recipes into gluten-free ones. A range of gluten-free white and bread flours is widely available from supermarkets and health food stores. (For all the gluten-free recipes in this book, where applicable, we used Doves Farm gluten-free flours, which gave excellent results. Other brands of gluten-free flours are also available.)

Alternatively, you can combine a selection of naturally gluten-free flours such as rice flour, gram (chickpea) flour, buckwheat flour, cornmeal or maize meal flour, tapioca flour and potato flour. Gluten-free bread mixes are also available from health food shops, and many of these are suitable for use in a breadmachine.

It is important to remember when making bread by hand or using a breadmachine that all utensils should be washed thoroughly before and after use, as even the slightest trace of wheat may cause an allergic reaction in someone who suffers with coeliac disease or who has an intolerance to wheat.

Yeast

Yeast is an essential ingredient in breadmaking as it causes the bread to rise. It is a living organism that feeds on the sugar and later the starches in the flour and it then releases a gas (carbon dioxide) that makes dough rise. Yeast is available in several different forms including fresh yeast, traditional or ordinary dried active yeast, and fast-action (quick) or easy blend (easy bake) dried yeast.

For this cookbook, in all relevant recipes, we have used fast-action dried yeast (also known as easy-blend, easy-bake or quick yeast). This type of yeast is recommended for use in a breadmachine and it is simple and convenient to use. Fresh yeast and traditional or ordinary dried active yeast (granules) are not suitable for use in a breadmachine.

Fast-action dried yeast

Fast-action dried yeast is a combination of dried yeast and the bread improver ascorbic acid (vitamin C), which accelerates the action of the yeast during the fermentation process. It is available in handy 6g or 7g (¼oz) sachets, or it can be bought in resealable foil packets of 125g (4½oz), which need to be kept in the refrigerator once opened and used within 10–12 weeks. Yeast won't work if it is stale, so always follow instructions for storage and adhere to the use-by date on the packet.

Other leavening ingredients

While yeast is the most common leavening ingredient used in breadmaking, other raising agents such as baking powder and bicarbonate of soda are also used for making some quick breads and teabreads in a breadmachine.

Liquids

The liquid used in breadmaking is usually water, although milk or a mixture of milk and water is used in some recipes. Other liquids, such as natural yogurt or eggs, may also be used in some breadmachine doughs. One main difference between making bread by hand and making bread in a breadmachine is the temperature of the water or liquid used. Whereas warm water or liquid is used when making bread by hand, cold water or cool milk (at room temperature) is usually required for breadmachine recipes (check your breadmachine manual for specific guidance on this) – unless using the "Rapid Bake" or "Fast Bake" programme, when warm water (or other liquid) may be required. If the timer-delay facility is being used, fresh milk should be replaced with dried skimmed milk powder and water, while eggs and other highly perishable ingredients should not be used.

Salt

Salt improves the flavour of bread and it also helps the dough to rise in a controlled and even way, resulting in a well-risen, even loaf. However, salt also slows down the action of yeast, so follow the quantities given and be careful not to add too much if you're adapting your own recipes.

Sugar and other sweeteners

Sugar helps to feed the yeast and make it more active, hence encouraging fermentation to take place more quickly, but too much sugar can impede the effectiveness of yeast. Modern types of yeast, including fast-action dried yeast, no longer need sugar as the flour provides them with enough food, but for good measure it is usual to add a little sugar in breadmachine recipes.

White, soft light brown and soft dark brown sugars can all be used in breadmachine recipes and in some recipes honey, golden syrup, maple syrup, malt extract, black treacle or molasses are used to add flavour and colour. Artificial sweeteners are not suitable for breadmaking.

Fats

Some breadmachine recipes include a little fat, such as butter or lard. Others may require the addition of oil or melted butter. Fats add flavour and richness, as well as improving the keeping qualities of the bread, but too much fat will slow down the action of the yeast. We have specified using butter in most of the recipes (where applicable), but in many cases you can use vegetable margarine or a similar alternative fat, if preferred. Low-fat spreads are not recommended for use in a breadmachine.

Bread mixes

There is a good range of bread mixes available, many of which are suitable for use in a breadmachine, and they are ideal for creating delicious home-baked breads with the minimum of fuss. They include white, wholemeal, granary, mixed grain and seed bread mixes as well as a range of flavoured varieties. Gluten-free bread mixes are also available.

Simply follow the instructions given on the packet and also refer to your manufacturer's instructions for more advice. Check that the weight of the ingredients in the packet does not exceed the total amount your breadmachine can handle, and check the consistency of the dough after 5 minutes, adding a little extra liquid if the mixture seems too dry.

Bread mixes are best baked immediately rather than using a timer-delay facility, as you cannot separate the yeast from the liquid.

breadmaking techniques

Please note that the following information is applicable only if you are using the "Dough" programme on your breadmachine. It does not apply to loaves that are made and baked completely in a breadmachine.

Knocking back and proving the dough

If you are using the "Dough" programme on your breadmachine, once this programme has finished, the dough is removed from the bread pan and then it is knocked back. This process will smooth out any large air pockets and ensure an even texture in the bread. To knock back the dough, turn it onto a lightly floured surface, then punch the risen dough with your fist to deflate it and knock out the air. Knead it briefly — for about 2–3 minutes — to redistribute the yeast and the gases formed by fermentation. Sometimes, at this stage, other ingredients such as olives, chopped herbs, chopped sun-dried tomatoes, chopped nuts, seeds or dried fruit may be kneaded into the dough (if they have not already been added during the "Dough" cycle).

The dough is then shaped or moulded as required, covered and left in a warm place until it has doubled in size. This is known as the proving stage. It is important not to over-prove the dough, otherwise the bread may collapse during baking — make sure the dough rises only until it is doubled in size. However, if it does not rise enough at this stage the loaf will be dense and flat. To test if the dough has risen enough, simply press it lightly with your fingertip. It should feel springy and the indentation made by your finger should slowly spring back and fill.

For professional-looking bread, proving baskets (often used by professional bakers) may be used for proving the dough. These are wicker baskets lined with linen or canvas, which are lightly floured, and they provide extra support to the bread during its final rising. They are available in round or long (baguette) shapes from good kitchenware shops. Once the dough has been proved in a basket, simply turn it out onto a baking sheet and bake as normal.

Shaping bread

If you are using the "Dough" programme on your breadmachine, once this programme has finished and you have knocked back the dough, it can be shaped by hand in various ways. Common shapes include cottage loaf, large round or oval, plait and baton. Dough can be formed into rolls of varying sizes and shapes including rounds, knots, long rolls and rings. Dough can also be slashed with a sharp knife in various ways before or after proving: slash the top of the loaf along its length; make criss-cross lines over the top of the loaf; cut a deep cross over the centre or cut several diagonal slashes across the top of the loaf.

Slashing the tops of loaves is done not only for visual effect but also for practical reasons, to provide escape routes for the air and to control the direction and extent of the rise during baking. The earlier you slash the dough, the wider the splits in the baked loaf; and the deeper the slashes, the more the bread will open during baking. Use a sharp knife and a swift, smooth action when slashing the dough, to avoid tearing it.

Glazing bread

If you are using the "Dough" programme on your breadmachine, once this programme has finished and you have knocked back and shaped the dough, brushing a loaf with a glaze before baking will enhance the colour of the bread, as well as adding flavour to the crust. Glazes not only help to give the baked bread an attractive finish, but they also add moisture to the loaf (by producing steam which helps to expand the loaf and ensure even cooking). Additionally, glazes help any toppings, garnishes or decorations that you may wish to add to loaves or rolls to stick to the surface of the dough, rather than falling off.

Breads may be glazed before (sometimes during) or just after baking. The most common ingredients used to glaze loaves are water, milk or beaten egg, but you can also try melted butter, olive oil, single cream, warmed clear honey, sugar syrup or a thin glacé icing for a variety of different finishes.

Finishing touches for bread

Once the dough has been shaped and glazed and before it is baked, various ingredients can be used for topping or finishing the bread, and each ingredient will create a different effect. Try sprinkling loaves or rolls with seeds, cracked or kibbled wheat, rolled oats, salt flakes, grated cheese or fresh herbs before baking, or dust with a little flour. For sweet breads, try dusting with icing sugar or sprinkling with sugar, chopped nuts, flaked almonds, dried fruits or grated chocolate, usually after baking.

Some enriched or speciality doughs may need covering to stop them browning too much during baking. If the bread begins to brown too quickly, cover it loosely with foil towards the end of the cooking time.

storing bread

Most home-made bread is at its best when served freshly baked and on the day it is made, and it should be eaten within 1–2 days as it stales quite quickly. Bread made from enriched doughs, with a high fat or sugar content, is also best eaten when freshly baked, but will keep longer, for up to 2–3 days.

Bread is best stored in a cool, dry, well-ventilated bread bin or an earthenware bread crock, and not in the refrigerator (the cold draws moisture out of the loaf, making it dry and stale). Wrap bread in foil or a polythene food bag if it has a soft crust, and in a paper or fabric bag if it is crusty.

Bread also freezes well for a short time – up to about 1 month. Simply seal the bread in a polythene freezer bag, or alternatively cut the loaf in half or into slices and freeze in convenient portions, ideal for defrosting when required. Defrost frozen breads at room temperature.

Quick and yeast-free breads tend to stale quickly and these are often best eaten freshly baked or within 1–2 days. Many shop-bought breads contain preservatives or flour improvers, hence they have a longer storage life than home-made breads.

breadmachines

There is a wide range of breadmachines to choose from and selecting a model to suit you will depend on several factors, including size or capacity required and budget. Do some research before buying a breadmachine to ensure it is the right model to suit you.

Breadmachines save time and effort and they are relatively simple to use. Before you begin, it is worth familiarising yourself with your machine and experimenting with the different programmes and options. Make a few basic breads given in your breadmachine manual before you try any new recipes. Practice makes perfect and you will soon have mastered how to use and programme your machine.

The names of the programmes used, such as "Rapid Bake" or "Basic White", may also differ slightly from one model to another. The delay-timer facility is useful for when you are not at home or are asleep – coming home or waking up to the smell of freshly baked bread is truly wonderful!

Programmes vary between models, but many include a "Basic White" or "Normal"; "Wholewheat" or "Wholemeal"; "Multigrain"; "Rapid Bake" or "Fast Bake"; "Sweet", "Raisin Bake" or "Raisin Beep"; "Dough"; "Raisin Dough"; and "Bake Only" programmes. Some models may also include more specialised programmes such as "French", "Cake", "Sandwich", "Pizza" and "Jam". Refer to your manufacturer's instruction manual for more details of the programmes included in your breadmachine.

Some breadmachines also offer a choice of three crust colours: light, medium or dark. However, if your machine does not have this option or you would prefer a darker crust once the loaf has been baked, simply brush the top of the baked loaf with a little melted butter, or egg yolk mixed with water, and brown under a hot grill or in a preheated oven at 200°C/400°F/gas mark 6 for 5–10 minutes.

Breadmachine pans vary in size between models and on large models you may have the option of making up to three different sizes of loaf. We have selected a medium-sized loaf for these recipes (where relevant), which should suit most breadmachines.

We have given ingredient quantities and cooking instructions for each recipe in this book, but it is very important that you read through your manufacturer's guidelines before embarking on any of the recipes. Breadmachines vary, so you may find, for example, that you have to add the ingredients to the bread pan in a slightly different order from that given in a recipe. Simply add the ingredients to the bread pan in the order specified in your instruction manual.

Useful tips when using a breadmachine

- Take the bread pan out of the machine before adding the ingredients. As well as making weighing out easier, it also avoids spillage in the breadmachine body.
- Accurate measuring is probably the most crucial factor for a successful loaf when using a breadmachine. Always use a proper set of measuring spoons. Many models include a measuring spoon and measuring cup for liquids, so use these if they are provided.

- It is important that the salt, sugar and yeast are kept separate from each other in the bread pan until mixing commences. This is less important if you are making some breads using the "Rapid Bake" or "Fast Bake" programme, as the ingredients are mixed as soon as the programme begins.

- Keep the yeast dry and separate from any liquids added to the bread pan until mixing commences. Separate the yeast from the liquid by adding the yeast before or after the flour (according to your instruction manual) – the flour acts as a temporary barrier between the yeast and liquid.

- Once the initial mixing cycle has begun, if you are able to, it is worth briefly lifting the lid and scraping down the sides of the bread pan using a flexible plastic or rubber spatula, to ensure even mixing, in case some of the ingredients stick to the corners of the bread pan.

- Once your breadmachine is in rising or baking mode, resist the temptation to open the lid, as the cold air will interfere with the temperature inside the machine and may slow things down. Some models incorporate a viewing window so that you can check on your bread's progress.

- When using the "Raisin Bake" or "Raisin Beep" programme, add extra ingredients and flavourings when the machine makes an audible sound or beep. Check that all the ingredients have mixed in and use a flexible plastic or rubber spatula to scrape down the sides of the bread pan, if necessary. If you do not have this facility on your machine, add the extra ingredients about 5 minutes before the end of the kneading cycle.

- If you are using the "Dough" programme, once this programme has finished and you have knocked back and shaped the dough, the shaped loaf or rolls should be placed on either a greased or a floured baking sheet(s) (or other tin) before baking. Some enriched or speciality breads are best baked on a greased rather than a floured baking sheet, to avoid sticking. With each recipe, we include guidelines on preparing the bread pan, baking sheets or other tins, where applicable.

- In some recipes, we use the "Bake Only" programme, which is ideal for "baking" recipes such as teabreads, tealoaves, cakes, etc. Many breadmachines include this programme but some don't, so choose these recipes only if your breadmachine includes this facility.

- When using the "Bake Only" programme (for example, when making teabreads or cakes), remove the kneading blade or paddle (if possible) from the bread pan before use. Grease and line the base of the bread pan with non-stick baking paper or greaseproof paper before adding the teabread (or cake) mixture. With some breadmachines, the kneading blade is a fixed part of the bread pan and cannot be removed.

- When using the "Bake Only" programme, remove the bread pan from the machine before transferring the teabread or cake mixture to the pan. Then place the bread pan back in position in the breadmachine before closing the lid and proceeding with the baking process.

- When using the "Bake Only" programme, set the timer, if possible, to the minimum time recommended in the recipe (or according to the manufacturer's instruction manual). Check the loaf after the shortest recommended time – and before the timer has finished, if necessary – and remove the baked loaf if it is ready. With some breadmachines, you can set the timer for as long as you wish (within reason), whilst on others the timer is preset to a specific amount of time – with some breadmachines this preset time can be reset immediately once the initial baking time has finished (if the recipe needs further baking time, for example), whilst with other models the timer cannot be reset straight away, so bear this in mind when choosing recipes to make in your particular breadmachine. Your manufacturer's guidelines should give you more advice about this.

- Even if you don't use the timer-delay facility on your breadmachine, the timer itself will be invaluable when you are making bread, so that you can see how many minutes are left to run on the programme.

- Don't touch the outside of the breadmachine during the baking cycle as it can sometimes get quite hot and may cause burns if you are not careful.

- Once the bread is baked, always take the bread pan out of the machine using oven gloves.

Gluten-free breads

When making gluten-free breads in a breadmachine, it is important to refer to the manufacturer's instructions for guidance on the specific programmes recommended. The "Rapid Bake" or "Fast Bake" programme will usually produce the best results.

Breadmachine recipes – trouble-shooting

Things can occasionally go wrong when making bread in a breadmachine and it is useful to know what may have gone wrong. Most, if not all, breadmachines include a trouble-shooting guide which details common errors, including problems with loaf size and shape, bread texture and crust colour and thickness, as well as bread-pan problems and operational errors. Please refer to your manufacturer's instruction manual for more details.

adapting recipes for use in a breadmachine

There is no easy formula for adapting conventional recipes for the breadmachine, but the best advice is to look through the recipes in this book to find one that is similar and use as a rough guide. It is also worth checking your manufacturer's instruction manual as this may give advice for adapting your own recipes to suit that particular model. Once you have tried a few recipes in your breadmachine, you will soon get the feel for how to adapt your own recipes.

Useful tips for adapting your own recipes

- First make sure you use the correct quantities for the breadmachine, ensuring that the total quantity of ingredients will fit into your bread pan. Do not exceed the recommended maximum. If necessary, reduce the flour and liquid quantities to match the quantities in a similar recipe.

- Use the flour and water quantities given in the recipes in this book as a guide and always refer to your manufacturer's instruction book. Keep the flour and liquid in the correct proportions. You may find that you need to add a little more water than the amount given in hand-made recipes, but this will vary depending on several factors such as the type of recipe itself, other ingredients used, etc. With a bit of practice, you will soon get the feel for approximately how much liquid to add to different basic quantities of flour.

- Always replace fresh yeast and traditional or ordinary dried active yeast (granules) with an appropriate amount of fast-action dried yeast (for more details refer to your manufacturer's guidelines). As a rough guide for wholemeal bread, try using 1 teaspoon fast-action dried yeast for up to 375g (13oz) flour or 1½ teaspoons fast-action dried yeast for up to 675g (1½lb) flour.

- If the timer-delay facility is being used, fresh milk should be replaced with dried skimmed milk powder and water, while eggs and other highly perishable ingredients should not be used.

- If your conventional recipe uses egg, include the egg as part of the total liquid measurement.

- Check the consistency of the dough during the first few minutes of mixing. Remember that breadmachines require a slightly softer dough than is needed for hand-made breads, so you may need to add a little extra liquid. The dough should be wet enough to relax back gradually. If the dough is crumbly or the machine seems to be labouring, add a little extra water. If the dough is sticking to the sides of the pan and doesn't form a ball, add a little extra flour.

basic & everyday breads

In this chapter you will find a selection of delicious breads that are ideal for regular baking. We include basic loaves, cobbs and plaits as well as a collection of slightly more unusual flavoured breads that are enjoyed all over the world, many on a daily basis.

Choose from rustic, homely bread recipes such as Garden Herb Bread, Honey Oatmeal Bread, Cottage Loaf, Milk Loaf and Flowerpot Breads. Or try authentic recipes from the rest of Europe and further afield such as French Bread, Pesto Whirl Bread or Greek Black Olive Bread, as well as Herby Polenta Bread, Caraway Seed Bread or Garlic Bubble Ring.

basic white bread (pictured left)

PREPARATION TIME 10 MINUTES   **COOKING TIME** VARIES ACCORDING TO BREADMACHINE

MAKES 1 LOAF (SERVES 10)

350ml (12fl oz / 1⅓ cups) water
500g (1lb 2oz / 3½ cups) strong plain white flour
1 tbsp skimmed milk powder
1½ tsp salt

2 tsp granulated sugar
25g (1oz) butter, diced
1 tsp fast-action dried yeast

1   Pour the water into the bread pan. Sprinkle over the flour, covering the water completely. Sprinkle the milk powder over the flour. Place the salt, sugar and butter in separate corners of the pan. Make a small indent in the centre of the flour and add the yeast.

2   Close the lid, set the machine to "Basic White"/"Normal" (or equivalent), then select the loaf size and crust type. Press Start.

3   After baking, remove the bread pan from the machine and turn the loaf out onto a wire rack to cool. Serve in slices.

basic brown bread

PREPARATION TIME 10 MINUTES   **COOKING TIME** VARIES ACCORDING TO BREADMACHINE

MAKES 1 LOAF (SERVES 10)

350ml (12fl oz / 1⅓ cups) water
250g (9oz / 1¾ cups) strong plain wholemeal flour
250g (9oz / 1¾ cups) strong plain white flour
1 tbsp skimmed milk powder

1½ tsp salt
2 tsp granulated sugar
25g (1oz) butter, diced
1 tsp fast-action dried yeast

1   Pour the water into the bread pan. Sprinkle over each type of flour in turn, covering the water completely. Sprinkle the milk powder over the flour. Place the salt, sugar and butter in separate corners of the pan. Make a small indent in the centre of the flour and add the yeast.

2   Close the lid, set the machine to "Basic White"/"Normal" or "Wholewheat" (or equivalent), then select the loaf size and crust type. Press Start.

3   After baking, remove the bread pan from the machine and turn the loaf out onto a wire rack to cool. Serve in slices.

cottage loaf

PREPARATION TIME 20 MINUTES, PLUS MIXING & KNEADING TIME IN BREADMACHINE, PLUS RISING & RESTING
COOKING TIME 30–35 MINUTES   **MAKES** 1 LOAF (SERVES 10–12)

325ml (11fl oz / 1⅓ cups) warm water (or according
    to bread-mix packet instructions)
500g (1lb 2oz) packet white bread mix

1 tsp salt
strong plain white flour, for dusting

1   Pour the water into the bread pan. (For a good-shaped cottage loaf, the dough needs to be firm
enough for the bottom round to support the top piece without sagging, so you may not need to add
all the water.) Sprinkle over the bread mix, covering the water completely. Close the lid, set the
machine to "Dough" and press Start.

2   Meanwhile, grease or flour 2 baking sheets and set aside. When the dough is ready, remove it from
the machine, knock it back on a lightly floured surface, then cut off one third of the dough. Shape
into plump balls and place each one on a baking sheet. Cover and leave to rise in a warm place until
doubled in size.

3   Preheat the oven to 220°C/425°F/gas mark 7. Gently flatten the balls of dough and carefully place
the smaller ball on top of the larger one. Gently push the floured handle of a wooden spoon down
through the centre of the dough to join the two pieces together, then slightly enlarge the hole with
your fingers. Leave to rest for 5–10 minutes.

4   Dissolve the salt in 1 tablespoon of hot water, then lightly brush over the loaf and dust with a little
flour. Using a sharp knife, make slashes around the top and base of the bread.

5   Bake for about 30–35 minutes, or until the bread is golden brown and sounds hollow when tapped
underneath. Transfer to a wire rack to cool. Serve in slices.

home-style wholemeal bread (pictured right)

PREPARATION TIME 10 MINUTES   **COOKING TIME** VARIES ACCORDING TO BREADMACHINE

MAKES 1 LOAF (SERVES 10)

350ml (12fl oz / 1⅓ cups) water
400g (14oz / 2¾ cups) strong plain wholemeal flour
115g (4oz / ¾ cup) strong plain white flour
1½ tsp salt

2 tsp granulated sugar
25g (1oz) butter, diced
1 tsp fast-action dried yeast

1   Pour the water into the bread pan. Sprinkle over each type of flour in turn, covering the water completely. Place the salt, sugar and butter in separate corners of the pan. Make a small indent in the centre of the flour and add the yeast.

2   Close the lid, set the machine to "Wholewheat" or "Multigrain" (or equivalent), then select the loaf size and crust type. Press Start.

3   After baking, remove the bread pan from the machine and turn the loaf out onto a wire rack to cool. Serve in slices.

farmhouse loaf

PREPARATION TIME 10 MINUTES   **COOKING TIME** VARIES ACCORDING TO BREADMACHINE

MAKES 1 LOAF (SERVES 10)

350ml (12fl oz / 1⅓ cups) water
400g (14oz / 2¾ cups) strong plain white flour, plus
     extra for dusting
115g (4oz / ¾ cup) strong plain wholemeal flour
1 tbsp skimmed milk powder

1½ tsp salt
2 tsp light soft brown sugar
25g (1oz) butter, diced
1½ tsp fast-action dried yeast

1   Pour the water into the bread pan. Sprinkle over each type of flour in turn, covering the water completely. Sprinkle the milk powder over the flour. Place the salt, sugar and butter in separate corners of the pan. Make a small indent in the centre of the flour and add the yeast.

2   Close the lid, set the machine to "Basic White"/"Normal"(or equivalent), then select the loaf size and crust type. Press Start. If possible, 10 minutes before the baking cycle starts, brush the top of the loaf with water and dust with a little flour. Using a sharp knife, cut a slash, about 1cm (½in) deep, along the length of the loaf.

3   After baking, remove the bread pan from the machine and turn the loaf out onto a wire rack to cool. Serve in slices.

honey oatmeal bread

PREPARATION TIME 15 MINUTES, PLUS MIXING & KNEADING TIME IN BREADMACHINE, PLUS RISING

COOKING TIME 30–35 MINUTES   **MAKES** 1 LOAF (SERVES 12–14)

250ml (9fl oz / 1 cup) water
100ml (3½fl oz / ⅓ cup) milk (at room temperature),
    plus extra for glazing
2 tbsp thick (set) honey
450g (1lb / 3 cups) strong plain brown flour

115g (4oz / 1 heaped cup) rolled oats,
    plus extra for sprinkling
1½ tsp salt
1 tsp granulated sugar
25g (1oz) butter, diced
1½ tsp fast-action dried yeast

1 Pour the water and milk into the bread pan, then add the honey. Sprinkle over the flour, covering the liquid completely. Sprinkle over the oats. Place the salt, sugar and butter in separate corners of the pan. Make a small indent in the centre and add the yeast. Close the lid, set the machine to "Dough" and press Start.

2 Grease or flour a baking sheet and set aside. When the dough is ready, remove it from the machine, knock it back on a lightly floured surface, then shape it into a round. Place on the baking sheet, cover and leave to rise in a warm place until doubled in size.

3 Preheat the oven to 230°C/450°F/gas mark 8. Slash the top of the loaf down the centre, brush with milk and sprinkle with oats.

4 Bake for 10 minutes, then reduce the oven temperature to 200°C/400°F/gas mark 6 and bake for a further 20–25 minutes, or until the bread is risen, lightly browned and sounds hollow when tapped underneath. Transfer to a wire rack to cool. Serve in slices.

malted wholegrain cobb

PREPARATION TIME 15 MINUTES, PLUS MIXING & KNEADING TIME IN BREADMACHINE, PLUS RISING
COOKING TIME 30–35 MINUTES   **MAKES** 1 LARGE LOAF (SERVES 14–16)

235ml (8½ fl oz / ¾ cup) water
100ml (3½ fl oz / ⅓ cup) milk (at room temperature),
    plus extra for glazing
2 tbsp malt extract
250g (9oz / 1¾ cups) strong Granary flour
250g (9oz / 1¾ cups) strong plain wholemeal flour

1½ tsp salt
2 tsp granulated sugar
25g (1oz) butter, diced
1½ tsp fast-action dried yeast
kibbled or cracked wheat, for sprinkling

1   Pour the water and milk into the bread pan, then add the malt extract. Sprinkle over each type of flour
    in turn, covering the liquid completely. Place the salt, sugar and butter in separate corners of the pan.
    Make a small indent in the centre of the flour and add the yeast. Close the lid, set the machine to
    "Dough" and press Start.

2   Grease or flour a baking sheet and set aside. When the dough is ready, remove it from the machine,
    knock it back on a lightly floured surface, then shape it into a large round. Place on the baking sheet,
    cover and leave to rise in a warm place until doubled in size.

3   Preheat the oven to 230°C/450°F/gas mark 8. Cut a cross shape into the top of the loaf, brush with a
    little milk and sprinkle with kibbled or cracked wheat.

4   Bake for 10 minutes, then reduce the oven temperature to 200°C/400°F/gas mark 6 and bake for a
    further 20–25 minutes, or until the bread is risen, lightly browned and sounds hollow when tapped
    underneath. Transfer to a wire rack to cool. Serve in slices.

french bread

PREPARATION TIME 15 MINUTES, PLUS MIXING & KNEADING TIME IN BREADMACHINE, PLUS RISING
COOKING TIME 15–20 MINUTES   **MAKES** 2 FRENCH STICKS (EACH LOAF SERVES 4–6)

300ml (½ pint / 1¼ cups) water
400g (14oz / 2¾ cups) strong plain white flour
55g (2oz / ½ cup) plain white flour

1½ tsp salt
1 tsp granulated sugar
1 tsp fast-action dried yeast

1   Pour the water into the bread pan. Sprinkle over each type of flour in turn, covering the water completely. Place the salt and sugar in separate corners of the pan. Make a small indent in the centre of the flour and add the yeast. Close the lid, set the machine to "French Dough" (or equivalent) and press Start.

2   Meanwhile, flour a large baking sheet and set aside. When the dough is ready, remove it from the machine and knock it back on a lightly floured surface. Divide the dough in half and roll out each portion to make a rectangle about 20 x 7.5cm (8 x 3in). Starting from a long edge, carefully roll up each rectangle of dough like a Swiss roll.

3   Gently roll and stretch each piece of dough to make a loaf about 28–33cm (11–13in) long. Place between the folds of a pleated tea towel for support, cover and leave to rise in a warm place until doubled in size.

4   Preheat the oven to 220°C/425°F/gas mark 7. Roll the loaves onto the baking sheet. Using a sharp knife, cut several diagonal slashes in the top of each loaf at regular intervals. Spray the inside of the hot oven with water, then immediately bake the loaves for 15–20 minutes, or until crisp and golden brown. Transfer to a wire rack to cool. Serve warm or cold.

caraway cheese loaf

PREPARATION TIME 15 MINUTES, PLUS MIXING & KNEADING TIME IN BREADMACHINE, PLUS RISING

COOKING TIME 30 MINUTES   **MAKES** 1 LOAF (SERVES 10–12)

300ml (½ pint / 1¼ cups) milk (at room temperature), plus extra for glazing
450g (1lb / 3 cups) strong plain white flour
2 tsp mustard powder
1 tbsp caraway seeds
25g (1oz) fresh Parmesan cheese, grated

115g (4oz / scant 1 cup) mature Cheddar cheese, finely grated
1¼ tsp salt
1½ tsp caster sugar
1½ tsp fast-action dried yeast

1   Pour the milk into the bread pan. Sprinkle over the flour, covering the milk completely, then sprinkle over the mustard powder, 2 teaspoons of the caraway seeds, the Parmesan cheese and 85g (3oz / ⅔ cup) of the Cheddar cheese. Place the salt and sugar in separate corners of the pan. Make a small indent in the centre of the flour and add the yeast. Close the lid, set the machine to "Dough" and press Start.

2   Meanwhile, grease or flour a baking sheet and set aside. When the dough is ready, remove it from the machine and knock it back on a lightly floured surface, then shape the dough into a 15cm (6in) round and place on the baking sheet. Cover and leave to rise in a warm place until doubled in size.

3   Preheat the oven to 230°C/450°F/gas mark 8. Using a sharp knife, cut a shallow cross in the top of the loaf, then brush with a little milk. Mix together the remaining caraway seeds and Cheddar cheese and sprinkle over the top of the loaf.

4   Bake the loaf for 10 minutes, then reduce the oven temperature to 200°C/400°F/gas mark 6 and bake for a further 20 minutes, or until the bread is risen, golden brown and sounds hollow when tapped underneath. Cover the loaf loosely with foil halfway through the cooking time if it is browning too much. Transfer to a wire rack to cool. Serve in slices.

caraway seed bread

PREPARATION TIME 10 MINUTES   **COOKING TIME** VARIES ACCORDING TO BREADMACHINE

MAKES 1 LOAF (SERVES 10)

350ml (12fl oz / 1⅓ cups) water
2 tbsp clear honey
400g (14oz / 2¾ cups) strong plain wholemeal flour
115g (4oz / ¾ cup) strong plain white flour
2 tbsp caraway seeds

2 tbsp skimmed milk powder
1½ tsp salt
25g (1oz) butter, diced
1 tsp fast-action dried yeast

1   Pour the water into the bread pan, then add the honey. Sprinkle over each type of flour in turn, covering the liquid completely. Sprinkle the caraway seeds over the flour, then sprinkle the milk powder over the seeds. Place the salt and butter in separate corners of the pan. Make a small indent in the centre of the flour and add the yeast.

2   Close the lid, set the machine to "Multigrain" or "Wholewheat" (or equivalent), then select the loaf size and crust type. Press Start.

3   After baking, remove the bread pan from the machine and turn the loaf out onto a wire rack to cool. Serve in slices.

Variations Use cumin or fennel seeds in place of caraway seeds. Use maple syrup in place of honey.

seeded rye bread

PREPARATION TIME 10 MINUTES   **COOKING TIME** VARIES ACCORDING TO BREADMACHINE

MAKES 1 LOAF (SERVES 10)

350ml (12fl oz / 1⅓ cups) water
1 tbsp clear honey
400g (14oz / 2¾ cups) strong plain white flour
115g (4oz / ¾ cup) rye flour
2 tbsp caraway seeds

2 tbsp skimmed milk powder
1½ tsp salt
25g (1oz) butter, diced
1 tsp fast-action dried yeast

1 Pour the water into the bread pan, then add the honey. Sprinkle over each type of flour in turn, covering the liquid completely. Sprinkle the caraway seeds over the flour, then sprinkle the milk powder over the seeds. Place the salt and butter in separate corners of the pan. Make a small indent in the centre of the flour and add the yeast.

2 Close the lid, set the machine to "Basic White"/"Normal" (or equivalent), then select the loaf size and crust type. Press Start.

3 After baking, remove the bread pan from the machine and turn the loaf out onto a wire rack to cool. Serve in slices.

sunflower seed loaf (pictured right)

PREPARATION TIME 10 MINUTES   **COOKING TIME** VARIES ACCORDING TO BREADMACHINE

MAKES 1 LOAF (SERVES 10)

300ml (½ pint / 1¼ cups) water
2 tbsp sunflower oil
225g (8oz / 1½ cups) strong plain white flour
225g (8oz / 1⅔ cups) strong Granary flour
1 tbsp skimmed milk powder

1½ tsp salt
2 tsp granulated sugar
1 tsp fast-action dried yeast
5 tbsp sunflower seeds

1 Pour the water into the bread pan, then add the oil. Sprinkle over each type of flour in turn, covering the liquid completely. Sprinkle the milk powder over the flour. Place the salt and sugar in separate corners of the pan. Make a small indent in the centre of the flour and add the yeast.

2 Close the lid, set the machine to "Basic White"/"Normal", with "Raisin", if available (or equivalent), then select the loaf size and crust type. Press Start.

3 Add the sunflower seeds when the machine makes a sound (beeps) to add extra ingredients during the kneading cycle (or add 5 minutes before the end of the kneading cycle).

4 After baking, remove the bread pan from the machine and turn the loaf out onto a wire rack to cool. Serve in slices.

six-seed bread

PREPARATION TIME 10 MINUTES   **COOKING TIME** VARIES ACCORDING TO BREADMACHINE

MAKES 1 LOAF (SERVES 10)

300ml (½ pint / 1¼ cups) water
2 tbsp sunflower oil
225g (8oz / 1½ cups) strong plain white flour
225g (8oz / 1⅔ cups) strong Granary flour
1 tbsp skimmed milk powder
1½ tsp salt
2 tsp granulated sugar

1 tsp fast-action dried yeast
2 tbsp sunflower seeds
1 tbsp pumpkin seeds
2 tsp sesame seeds
2 tsp poppy seeds
1 tsp caraway seeds
1 tsp cumin or fennel seeds

1   Pour the water into the bread pan, then add the oil. Sprinkle over each type of flour in turn, covering the liquid completely. Sprinkle the milk powder over the flour. Place the salt and sugar in separate corners of the pan. Make a small indent in the centre of the flour and add the yeast.

2   Close the lid, set the machine to "Basic White"/"Normal", with "Raisin", if available (or equivalent), then select the loaf size and crust type. Press Start.

3   Combine the seeds. Add the mixed seeds when the machine makes a sound (beeps) to add extra ingredients during the kneading cycle (or add 5 minutes before the end of the kneading cycle).

4   After baking, remove the bread pan from the machine and turn the loaf out onto a wire rack to cool. Serve in slices.

Variation Packets of prepared mixed seeds suitable for bread-making are available. Use 5 tablespoons ready-mixed seeds in place of the seeds listed above.

cheese & sesame seed cobb

PREPARATION TIME 15 MINUTES, PLUS MIXING & KNEADING TIME IN BREADMACHINE, PLUS RISING
COOKING TIME 35–45 MINUTES   **MAKES** 1 LOAF (SERVES 10)

300ml (½ pint / 1¼ cups) milk (at room
    temperature), plus extra for glazing
450g (1lb / 3 cups) strong plain white flour
2 tsp mustard powder
a few turns of freshly ground black pepper
85g (3oz / ⅔ cup) Gruyère or Emmental cheese,
    finely grated

1¼ tsp salt
1½ tsp caster sugar
25g (1oz) butter, diced
1½ tsp fast-action dried yeast
sesame seeds, for sprinkling

1   Pour the milk into the bread pan. Sprinkle over the flour, covering the milk completely, then sprinkle
    over the mustard powder, black pepper and cheese. Place the salt, sugar and butter in separate
    corners of the pan. Make a small indent in the centre of the flour and add the yeast. Close the lid, set
    the machine to "Dough" and press Start.

2   Meanwhile, grease or flour a baking sheet and set aside. When the dough is ready, remove it from
    the machine and knock it back on a lightly floured surface, then shape the dough into a round cobb
    and place on the baking sheet. Cover and leave to rise in a warm place until doubled in size.

3   Preheat the oven to 190°C/375°F/gas mark 5. Lightly brush the top of the loaf with milk and
    sprinkle with sesame seeds.

4   Bake for 35–45 minutes, or until the bread is risen, golden brown and sounds hollow when
    tapped underneath. Transfer to a wire rack to cool. Serve in slices.

garden herb bread

PREPARATION TIME 10 MINUTES   **COOKING TIME** VARIES ACCORDING TO BREADMACHINE

MAKES 1 LOAF (SERVES 10)

350ml (12fl oz / 1⅓ cups) water
500g (1lb 2oz / 3½ cups) strong plain white flour
1 tbsp skimmed milk powder
2 tbsp chopped fresh parsley
2 tbsp chopped fresh chives

2 tsp chopped fresh thyme
1½ tsp salt
2 tsp granulated sugar
25g (1oz) butter, diced
1 tsp fast-action dried yeast

1 Pour the water into the bread pan. Sprinkle over the flour, covering the water completely. Sprinkle the milk powder over the flour. Combine the herbs, then sprinkle them over the milk powder. Place the salt, sugar and butter in separate corners of the pan. Make a small indent in the centre of the flour and add the yeast.

2 Close the lid, set the machine to "Basic White"/"Normal" (or equivalent), then select the loaf size and crust type. Press Start.

3 After baking, remove the bread pan from the machine and turn the loaf out onto a wire rack to cool. Serve in slices.

Variation Use 2 tablespoons chopped fresh coriander or basil in place of the thyme.

malted wheat bread (pictured right)

PREPARATION TIME 10 MINUTES   **COOKING TIME** VARIES ACCORDING TO BREADMACHINE
MAKES 1 LOAF (SERVES 10)

300ml (½ pint / 1¼ cups) water
2 tbsp malt extract
450g (1lb / 3¼ cups) strong Granary flour
1 tbsp skimmed milk powder

1½ tsp salt
2 tsp granulated sugar
25g (1oz) butter, diced
1 tsp fast-action dried yeast

1 Pour the water into the bread pan, then add the malt extract. Sprinkle over the flour, covering the liquid completely. Sprinkle the milk powder over the flour. Place the salt, sugar and butter in separate corners of the pan. Make a small indent in the centre of the flour and add the yeast.

2 Close the lid, set the machine to "Wholewheat" or "Multigrain" (or equivalent), then select the loaf size and crust type. Press Start.

3 After baking, remove the bread pan from the machine and turn the loaf out onto a wire rack to cool. Serve in slices.

granary herb loaf

PREPARATION TIME 10 MINUTES
COOKING TIME VARIES ACCORDING TO BREADMACHINE   **MAKES** 1 LOAF (SERVES 8–10)

300ml (½ pint / 1¼ cups) water
450g (1lb / 3¼ cups) strong malted Granary flour
1 tbsp skimmed milk powder
1 tbsp chopped fresh mixed herbs,
    such as chives, sage and marjoram
1 tbsp chopped fresh parsley

1½ tsp freshly ground black pepper
2 tsp salt
2 tsp caster sugar
25g (1oz) butter, diced
1½ tsp fast-action dried yeast

1 Pour the water into the bread pan. Sprinkle over the flour, covering the water completely. Sprinkle the milk powder over the flour. Combine the herbs and black pepper, then sprinkle these over the milk powder. Place the salt, sugar and butter in separate corners of the pan. Make a small indent in the centre of the flour and add the yeast.

2 Close the lid, set the machine to "Wholewheat" (or equivalent), then select the loaf size and crust type. Press Start.

3 After baking, remove the bread pan from the machine and turn the loaf out onto a wire rack to cool. Serve in slices.

flowerpot breads

PREPARATION TIME 15 MINUTES, PLUS MIXING & KNEADING TIME IN BREADMACHINE, PLUS RISING

COOKING TIME 30–40 MINUTES   **MAKES** 2 LOAVES (EACH LOAF SERVES 4)

315ml (10½fl oz / 1¼ cups) water
1 tbsp malt extract
450g (1lb / 3 cups) strong plain brown flour
55g (2oz / ⅓ cup) barley flakes,
    plus extra for sprinkling
1–2 tbsp chopped fresh mixed herbs

1½ tsp salt
2 tsp caster sugar
25g (1oz) butter, diced
2 tsp fast-action dried yeast
milk, for glazing

1   Liberally brush 2 new terracotta flowerpots (about 14cm/5½in in diameter and 12cm/4½in high) with vegetable oil, inside and out, then bake in a hot oven (200°C/400°F/gas mark 6) for about 30 minutes. Leave to cool, then repeat this process until the pots are impregnated with oil. Do not wash after use: wipe clean with kitchen paper. Lightly grease the pots and set aside.

2   Pour the water into the bread pan and add the malt extract. Sprinkle over the flour, covering the liquid completely, then sprinkle over the barley flakes and herbs. Place the salt, sugar and butter in separate corners of the pan. Make a small indent in the centre of the flour and add the yeast. Close the lid, set the machine to "Dough" and press Start.

3   When the dough is ready, remove it from the machine, knock it back on a lightly floured surface and divide in half. Shape and fit each piece of dough into a flowerpot – the dough should roughly half-fill the pot.

4   Cover and leave to rise in a warm place for 45–60 minutes, or until the dough almost reaches the top of the flowerpots.

5   Preheat the oven to 200°C/400°F/gas mark 6. Brush the loaf tops with a little milk and sprinkle with barley flakes. Bake for about 30–40 minutes, or until the bread is risen and sounds hollow when turned out and tapped underneath. Place on a wire rack to cool. Serve in slices.

herb flutes

PREPARATION TIME 15 MINUTES, PLUS MIXING & KNEADING TIME IN BREADMACHINE, PLUS RISING
COOKING TIME 25 MINUTES   **MAKES** 2 LOAVES (EACH LOAF SERVES 4–6)

275ml (9½fl oz /1 cup) water
2 tbsp olive oil
450g (1lb / 3 cups) strong plain white flour,
    plus extra for dusting
1 tbsp dried herbes de Provence

55g (2oz / ⅓ cup) fresh Parmesan cheese, grated
1¼ tsp salt
1½ tsp caster sugar
1½ tsp fast-action dried yeast

1   Pour the water into the bread pan, then add the oil. Sprinkle over the flour, covering the liquid
    completely, then sprinkle over the dried herbs and cheese. Place the salt and sugar in separate
    corners of the pan. Make a small indent in the centre of the flour and add the yeast. Close the lid, set
    the machine to "Dough" and press Start.

2   Meanwhile, grease or flour a large baking sheet and set aside. When the dough is ready, remove it
    from the machine, knock it back on a lightly floured surface, then divide it in half and shape each half
    into a baton about 30cm (12in) in length. Place on the baking sheet, cover and leave to rise in a warm
    place for about 45 minutes, or until doubled in size.

3   Preheat the oven to 220°C/425°F/gas mark 7. Dust each loaf with a little flour, then, using a sharp
    knife, slash across the top of each loaf 4 times diagonally at regular intervals.

4   Bake for about 25 minutes, or until the bread is risen, golden brown and sounds hollow when tapped
    underneath. Transfer to a wire rack to cool. Serve warm or cold.

milk loaf

PREPARATION TIME 10 MINUTES   **COOKING TIME** VARIES ACCORDING TO BREADMACHINE
MAKES 1 LOAF (SERVES 10)

200ml (7fl oz / ¾ cup) milk (at room temperature)
100ml (3½fl oz / ⅓ cup) water
450g (1lb / 3 cups) strong plain white flour
1½ tsp salt

2 tsp granulated sugar
25g (1oz) butter, diced
1 tsp fast-action dried yeast

1   Pour the milk and water into the bread pan. Sprinkle over the flour, covering the liquid completely.
    Place the salt, sugar and butter in separate corners of the pan. Make a small indent in the centre of
    the flour and add the yeast.
2   Close the lid, set the machine to "Basic White"/"Normal" (or equivalent), then select the loaf size
    and crust type. Press Start.
3   After baking, remove the bread pan from the machine and turn the loaf out onto a wire rack to cool.
    Serve in slices.

barley bread

PREPARATION TIME 15 MINUTES, PLUS MIXING & KNEADING TIME IN BREADMACHINE, PLUS RISING
COOKING TIME 30–35 MINUTES   **MAKES** 1 LOAF (SERVES 10–12)

350ml (12fl oz / 1⅓ cups) water
400g (14oz / 2¾ cups) strong plain brown flour
115g (4oz / 1 cup) barley flour

2 tsp salt
2 tsp caster sugar
1½ tsp fast-action dried yeast

1   Pour the water into the bread pan. Sprinkle over each type of flour in turn, covering the water completely. Place the salt and sugar in separate corners of the pan. Make a small indent in the centre of the flour and add the yeast. Close the lid, set the machine to "Dough" and press Start.

2   Meanwhile, grease a 900g (2lb) loaf tin and set aside. When the dough is ready, remove it from the machine, knock it back on a lightly floured surface, then shape the dough into an oblong. Place in the loaf tin, cover and leave to rise in a warm place until doubled in size.

3   Preheat the oven to 230°C/450°F/gas mark 8. Bake for 10 minutes, then reduce the oven temperature to 200°C/400°F/gas mark 6 and bake for a further 20–25 minutes, or until the bread is risen, lightly browned and sounds hollow when turned out and tapped underneath. Cool on a wire rack. Serve in slices.

sun-dried tomato bread (pictured left)

PREPARATION TIME 10 MINUTES   **COOKING TIME** VARIES ACCORDING TO BREADMACHINE
MAKES 1 LOAF (SERVES 8–10)

300ml (½ pint / 1¼ cups) water
1 tbsp oil from a jar of sun-dried tomatoes
450g (1lb / 3 cups) strong plain white flour
55g (2oz / ⅓ cup) fresh Parmesan cheese,
    finely grated

1½ tsp salt
2 tsp caster sugar
1 tsp fast-action dried yeast
55g (2oz / ½ cup) sun-dried tomatoes in oil
    (drained weight), patted dry and chopped

1   Pour the water into the bread pan, then add the oil. Sprinkle over the flour, covering the liquid completely. Sprinkle over the Parmesan cheese. Place the salt and sugar in separate corners of the pan. Make a small indent in the centre of the flour and add the yeast.

2   Close the lid, set the machine to "Basic White"/"Normal", with "Raisin", if available (or equivalent), then select the loaf size and crust type. Press Start.

3   Add the sun-dried tomatoes when the machine makes a sound (beeps) to add extra ingredients during the kneading cycle (or add 5 minutes before the end of the kneading cycle).

4   After baking, remove the bread pan from the machine and turn the loaf out onto a wire rack to cool. Serve in slices.

pesto whirl bread

PREPARATION TIME 20 MINUTES, PLUS MIXING & KNEADING TIME IN BREADMACHINE, PLUS RISING
COOKING TIME 25–30 MINUTES   **MAKES** 1 LOAF (SERVES 10–12)

325ml (11fl oz / 1⅓ cups) water
2 tbsp olive oil
500g (1lb 2oz / 3½ cups) strong plain white flour
1 tsp salt

1 tsp caster sugar
1 tsp fast-action dried yeast
4 tbsp ready-made green pesto sauce

1   Pour the water into the bread pan, then add the oil. Sprinkle over the flour, covering the liquid completely. Place the salt and sugar in separate corners of the pan. Make a small indent in the centre of the flour and add the yeast. Close the lid, set the machine to "Dough" and press Start.

2   Meanwhile, grease a 900g (2lb) loaf tin and set aside. When the dough is ready, remove it from the machine, knock it back on a lightly floured surface, then roll or pat out to form a rectangle about 30 x 20cm (12 x 8in) in size.

3   Spread the pesto evenly over the rectangle of dough, then roll up the dough fairly tightly like a Swiss roll, starting from a short side. Re-shape slightly if necessary and place in the loaf tin. Cover and leave to rise in a warm place for about 30–45 minutes, or until doubled in size.

4   Preheat the oven to 220°C/425°F/gas mark 7. Bake for 25–30 minutes, or until the loaf is risen and golden. Turn out and cool on a wire rack. Serve in slices on its own or spread with butter.

Variation   Use ready-made red pesto sauce in place of traditional green pesto sauce.

greek black olive bread

PREPARATION TIME 20 MINUTES, PLUS MIXING & KNEADING TIME IN BREADMACHINE, PLUS RISING
COOKING TIME 30–35 MINUTES   **MAKES** 1 LOAF (SERVES 10–12)

325ml (11fl oz / 1⅓ cups) water
2 tbsp extra-virgin olive oil
500g (1lb 2oz / 3½ cups) strong plain white flour,
    plus extra for dusting

1 tsp salt
1 tsp granulated sugar
1 tsp fast-action dried yeast
115g (4oz / ¾ cup) pitted black olives
    (drained weight), chopped

1   Pour the water into the bread pan, then add the oil. Sprinkle over the flour, covering the liquid
    completely. Place the salt and sugar in separate corners of the pan. Make a small indent in the centre
    of the flour and add the yeast. Close the lid, set the machine to "Dough" and press Start.

2   Meanwhile, grease or flour a baking sheet and set aside. When the dough is ready, remove it from
    the machine, knock it back on a lightly floured surface, then knead in about half of the chopped olives.
    Roll out to form a rectangle about 35 x 25cm (14 x 10in).

3   Sprinkle the surface of the dough evenly with the remaining olives, then roll up fairly tightly like a
    Swiss roll, starting from a short side. Pinch the edges of each end together to seal. Place the loaf,
    seam-side down, on the baking sheet. Cover and leave to rise in a warm place until doubled in size.

4   Preheat the oven to 220°C/425°F/gas mark 7. Dust the loaf with a little sifted flour. Bake for
    10 minutes, then reduce the oven temperature to 190°C/375°F/gas mark 5 and bake for a further
    20–25 minutes, or until the bread is risen, golden brown and sounds hollow when tapped underneath.
    Transfer to a wire rack to cool. Serve warm or cold in slices.

plaited herb bread

PREPARATION TIME 20 MINUTES, PLUS MIXING & KNEADING TIME IN BREADMACHINE, PLUS RISING

COOKING TIME 35 45 MINUTES   **MAKES** 1 LOAF (SERVES 10)

150ml (¼ pint / ⅔ cup) water
150ml (¼ pint / ⅔ cup) milk (at room
    temperature), plus extra for glazing
450g (1lb / 3 cups) strong plain white flour
1 tbsp dried herbes de Provence

85g (3oz / ⅔ cup) mature Cheddar or red Leicester
    cheese, finely grated
1¼ tsp salt
1½ tsp caster sugar
25g (1oz) butter, diced
1½ tsp fast-action dried yeast

1   Pour the water and milk into the bread pan. Sprinkle over the flour, covering the liquid completely,
    then sprinkle over the dried herbs and cheese. Place the salt, sugar and butter in separate corners
    of the pan. Make a small indent in the centre of the flour and add the yeast. Close the lid, set the
    machine to "Dough" and press Start.

2   Meanwhile, grease or flour a baking sheet and set aside. When the dough is ready, remove it from
    the machine, knock it back on a lightly floured surface, then divide it in half. Roll each piece of dough
    into a long sausage or rope shape. Place them side by side and pinch together at one end to seal.

3   Loosely plait the ropes of dough together, then pinch them together at the other end. Place the plait
    on the baking sheet. Cover and leave to rise in a warm place until doubled in size.

4   Preheat the oven to 190°C/375°F/gas mark 5. Lightly brush the plait with milk. Bake for 35–45
    minutes, or until the bread is risen, golden brown and sounds hollow when tapped underneath.
    Transfer to a wire rack to cool. Serve in slices.

cheese & poppyseed plait

PREPARATION TIME 15 MINUTES, PLUS MIXING & KNEADING TIME IN BREADMACHINE, PLUS RISING
COOKING TIME 30–40 MINUTES   **MAKES** 1 LOAF (SERVES 10)

300ml (½ pint / 1¼ cups) milk (at room temperature),
    plus extra for glazing
450g (1lb / 3 cups) strong plain white flour
2 tsp mustard powder
a few turns of freshly ground black pepper
85g (3oz / ⅔ cup) mature Cheddar cheese, finely grated

1¼ tsp salt
1½ tsp caster sugar
25g (1oz) butter, diced
1½ tsp fast-action dried yeast
poppy seeds, for sprinkling

1   Pour the milk into the bread pan. Sprinkle over the flour, covering the milk completely, then sprinkle
    over the mustard powder, black pepper and cheese. Place the salt, sugar and butter in separate
    corners of the pan. Make a small indent in the centre of the flour and add the yeast. Close the lid, set
    the machine to "Dough" and press Start.

2   Meanwhile, grease or flour a baking sheet and set aside. When the dough is ready, remove it from
    the machine, knock it back on a lightly floured surface, then divide it in half. Roll each piece of dough
    into a long sausage or rope shape. Pinch them together at one end to seal.

3   Loosely plait the ropes of dough together, then pinch them together at the other end. Place the plait
    on the baking sheet. Cover and leave to rise in a warm place until doubled in size.

4   Preheat the oven to 190°C/375°F/gas mark 5. Brush the plait with a little milk and sprinkle with
    poppy seeds.

5   Bake for 30–40 minutes, or until the bread is risen, golden brown and sounds hollow when tapped
    underneath. Transfer to a wire rack to cool. Serve in slices.

cheese & grain cobb

PREPARATION TIME 15 MINUTES, PLUS MIXING & KNEADING TIME IN BREADMACHINE, PLUS RISING
COOKING TIME 35–45 MINUTES   **MAKES** 1 LOAF (SERVES 10–12)

300ml (½ pint / 1¼ cups) milk (at room
   temperature), plus extra for glazing
450g (1lb / 3¼ cups) strong Granary flour
2 tsp mustard powder
a few turns of freshly ground black pepper
85g (3oz / ⅔ cup) red Leicester or mature Cheddar
   cheese, finely grated

1½ tsp salt
1½ tsp granulated sugar
25g (1oz) butter, diced
1½ tsp fast-action dried yeast
kibbled or cracked wheat, for sprinkling

1   Pour the milk into the bread pan. Sprinkle over the flour, covering the milk completely, then sprinkle
    over the mustard powder, black pepper and cheese. Place the salt, sugar and butter in separate
    corners of the pan. Make a small indent in the centre of the flour and add the yeast. Close the lid, set
    the machine to "Dough" and press Start.

2   Meanwhile, grease or flour a baking sheet and set aside. When the dough is ready, remove it from
    the machine and knock it back on a lightly floured surface, then shape the dough into a round cobb
    and place on the baking sheet. Cover and leave to rise in a warm place for 30–45 minutes, or until
    doubled in size.

3   Preheat the oven to 190°C/375°F/gas mark 5. Lightly brush the top of the loaf with milk, then sprinkle
    with kibbled or cracked wheat.

4   Bake for 35–45 minutes, or until the bread is risen, golden brown and sounds hollow when tapped
    underneath. Transfer to a wire rack to cool. Serve in slices.

garlic bubble ring

PREPARATION TIME 20 MINUTES, PLUS MIXING & KNEADING TIME IN BREADMACHINE, PLUS RISING
COOKING TIME 30–40 MINUTES   **MAKES** 1 LOAF (SERVES 12)

325ml (11fl oz / 1⅓ cups) warm water (or according to bread-mix packet instructions)
500g (1lb 2oz) packet white bread mix
100g (3½oz) butter, melted
1 egg, beaten

25g (1oz) fresh Parmesan cheese, finely grated
2 cloves garlic, crushed
½ tsp salt
1 tsp dried Italian herb seasoning

1   Pour the correct amount of water into the bread pan. Sprinkle over the bread mix, covering the water completely. Close the lid, set the machine to "Dough" and press Start. Meanwhile, grease a 23cm (9in) loose-bottomed springform tin fitted with a tube base, or a ring mould, and set aside.

2   When the dough is ready, remove it from the machine, knock it back on a lightly floured surface, then divide it into 12 equal portions and roll each piece into a ball.

3   Combine the melted butter, egg, cheese, garlic, salt and dried herbs in a small bowl, mixing well. Dip the dough balls into the mixture, coating them liberally all over, then arrange them in a single layer in the tin. Drizzle over any remaining butter mixture. Cover and leave to rise in a warm place until doubled in size.

4   Preheat the oven to 190°C/375°F/gas mark 5. Bake for 30–40 minutes, or until the bread is risen and golden brown. Turn out and cool on a wire rack. Pull the rolls apart to serve warm or cold.

cheese & olive bread

PREPARATION TIME 10 MINUTES   **COOKING TIME** VARIES ACCORDING TO BREADMACHINE

MAKES 1 LOAF (SERVES 8–10)

300ml (½ pint / 1¼ cups) water
1 tbsp extra-virgin olive oil
450g (1lb / 3 cups) strong plain white flour
70g (2½oz / ½ cup) fresh Parmesan cheese,
    finely grated
2 tsp dried Italian herb seasoning

1½ tsp salt
2 tsp caster sugar
1 tsp fast-action dried yeast
55g (2oz / ⅓ cup) mixed pitted black
    and green olives, chopped

1   Pour the water into the bread pan, then add the oil. Sprinkle over the flour, covering the liquid
    completely. Sprinkle over the Parmesan cheese and dried herb seasoning. Place the salt and sugar
    in separate corners of the pan. Make a small indent in the centre of the flour and add the yeast.

2   Close the lid, set the machine to "Basic White"/"Normal", with "Raisin", if available (or equivalent),
    then select the loaf size and crust type. Press Start.

3   Add the mixed olives when the machine makes a sound (beeps) to add extra ingredients during
    the kneading cycle (or add 5 minutes before the end of the kneading cycle).

4   After baking, remove the bread pan from the machine and turn the loaf out onto a wire rack to cool.
    Serve in slices.

golden cheesy breads

PREPARATION TIME 15 MINUTES, PLUS MIXING & KNEADING TIME IN BREADMACHINE, PLUS RISING
COOKING TIME 20–25 MINUTES   **MAKES** 4 SMALL LOAVES (EACH LOAF SERVES 1–2)

300ml (½ pint / 1¼ cups) milk (at room
    temperature), plus extra for glazing
450g (1lb / 3 cups) strong plain white flour
1 tsp mustard powder
200g (7oz / 1⅔ cups) Gouda cheese, grated

1¼ tsp salt
1½ tsp caster sugar
25g (1oz) butter, diced
1½ tsp fast-action dried yeast

1   Pour the milk into the bread pan. Sprinkle over the flour, covering the milk completely, then sprinkle
    over the mustard powder and two-thirds of the cheese. Place the salt, sugar and butter in separate
    corners of the pan. Make a small indent in the centre of the flour and add the yeast. Close the lid, set
    the machine to "Dough" and press Start.

2   Meanwhile, grease or flour 2 baking sheets and set aside. When the dough is ready, remove it from
    the machine, knock it back on a lightly floured surface, then divide into 4 equal portions. Shape each
    portion into a round or oval and place on the baking sheets. Cover and leave to rise in a warm place
    until doubled in size.

3   Preheat the oven to 200°C/400°F/gas mark 6. Lightly brush the tops of the loaves with a little milk,
    then sprinkle over the remaining cheese.

4   Bake for 20–25 minutes, or until the bread is risen and golden brown and sounds hollow when
    tapped underneath. Cover the loaves loosely with foil towards the end of the cooking time if they
    are browning too much. Transfer to a wire rack to cool.

sesame ring breads

PREPARATION TIME 15 MINUTES, PLUS MIXING & KNEADING TIME IN BREADMACHINE, PLUS RISING
COOKING TIME 10–15 MINUTES   **MAKES** 8 RING BREADS

250ml (9fl oz / 1 cup) water
3 tbsp unrefined or cold-pressed sesame oil
1 tbsp clear honey
450g (1lb / 3 cups) strong plain white flour
1½ tsp salt

2 tsp caster sugar
1 sachet (7g / ¼oz) fast-action dried yeast
beaten egg, for glazing
sesame seeds, for sprinkling

1   Pour the water into a bowl, add the oil and honey and whisk well. Pour the mixture into the bread pan. Sprinkle over the flour, covering the liquid completely. Place the salt and sugar in separate corners of the pan. Make a small indent in the centre of the flour and add the yeast. Close the lid, set the machine to "Dough" and press Start.

2   Meanwhile, grease or flour 2 baking sheets and set aside. When the dough is ready, remove it from the machine, knock it back on a lightly floured surface, then divide it into 8 equal portions.

3   Roll each portion into a sausage or rope shape about 30cm (12in) long. Form each rope of dough into a ring and press the ends firmly together to seal. Place on the baking sheets, spacing them well apart. Cover and leave to rise in a warm place until doubled in size.

4   Preheat the oven to 200°C/400°F/gas mark 6. Lightly brush the dough rings with a little beaten egg and sprinkle with sesame seeds.

5   Bake for about 10–15 minutes, or until risen and golden brown. Transfer to a wire rack to cool. Serve warm.

herby polenta bread

PREPARATION TIME 10 MINUTES   **COOKING TIME** VARIES ACCORDING TO BREADMACHINE

MAKES 1 LOAF (SERVES 10)

300ml (½ pint / 1¼ cups) water
3 tbsp clear honey
3 tbsp chopped fresh mixed herbs,
    such as flat-leaf parsley, chives and basil
55g (2oz / ⅓ cup) polenta

350g (12oz / 2½ cups) strong plain wholemeal flour
115g (4oz / ¾ cup) strong plain white flour
1½ tsp salt
25g (1oz) butter, diced
1½ tsp fast-action dried yeast

1   Pour the water into the bread pan, then add the honey. Sprinkle over the chopped herbs and polenta, then sprinkle over each type of flour in turn, covering the liquid completely.

2   Place the salt and butter in separate corners of the pan. Make a small indent in the centre of the flour and add the yeast.

3   Close the lid, set the machine to "Wholewheat" (or equivalent), then select the loaf size and crust type. Press Start.

4   After baking, remove the bread pan from the machine and turn the loaf out onto a wire rack to cool. Serve in slices.

Variation Use maple syrup in place of honey.

cheese & bacon bread

PREPARATION TIME 20 MINUTES   **COOKING TIME** VARIES ACCORDING TO BREADMACHINE

MAKES 1 LOAF (SERVES 10)

350ml (12fl oz / 1⅓ cups) water
500g (1lb 2oz / 3½ cups) strong plain brown flour
1½ tbsp skimmed milk powder
1½ tsp salt
1 tbsp granulated sugar

1 tsp fast-action dried yeast
85g (3oz / ⅓ cup) cold cooked lean smoked
    back bacon, chopped
85g (3oz / ⅔ cup) mature
    Cheddar cheese, grated

1   Pour the water into the bread pan. Sprinkle over the flour, covering the water completely.
    Sprinkle the milk powder over the flour. Place the salt and sugar in separate corners of the pan.
    Make a small indent in the centre of the flour and add the yeast.

2   Close the lid, set the machine to "Basic White"/"Normal", with "Raisin", if available (or equivalent),
    then select the loaf size and crust type. Press Start.

3   Combine the bacon and cheese. Add the bacon and cheese mixture when the machine makes a
    sound (beeps) to add extra ingredients during the kneading cycle (or add 5 minutes before the end
    of the kneading cycle).

4   After baking, remove the bread pan from the machine and turn the loaf out onto a wire rack to cool.
    Serve in slices.

sausage & salsa popovers

PREPARATION TIME 20 MINUTES, PLUS MIXING & KNEADING TIME IN BREADMACHINE, PLUS RISING
COOKING TIME 15–20 MINUTES   **MAKES** 10 POPOVERS

325ml (11fl oz / 1⅓ cups) warm water
   (or according to bread-mix packet instructions)
500g (1lb 2oz) packet white bread mix
55g (2oz / ½ cup) mature Cheddar cheese,
   finely grated

a good pinch of cayenne pepper
10 cold cooked skinless thick sausages
   of your choice (pork, beef, herby, spicy, etc.)
20 tsp tomato salsa (2 tsp per popover)
beaten egg, for glazing

1   Pour the correct amount of water into the bread pan. Sprinkle over the bread mix, covering the water completely, then sprinkle over the cheese and cayenne pepper. Close the lid, set the machine to "Dough" and press Start.

2   Meanwhile, grease or flour 2 baking sheets and set aside. When the dough is ready, remove it from the machine and knock it back on a lightly floured surface. Roll out the dough to form a 50 x 20cm (20 x 8in) rectangle, then cut into ten 10cm (4in) squares.

3   Place 1 sausage diagonally across 1 square of dough, then spread 2 teaspoons of salsa over the sausage. Fold the remaining two corners of the dough square over the sausage, pinching the edges together and pressing them down gently to seal (you will still be able to see both ends of the sausage).

4   Repeat with the remaining dough squares, sausages and salsa, to make a total of 10 popovers. Place, seam-side up, on the baking sheets, cover and leave to rise in a warm place for about 30 minutes, or until doubled in size.

5   Preheat the oven to 200°C/400°F/gas mark 6. Lightly brush the popovers with a little beaten egg, then bake for 15–20 minutes, or until risen and golden brown. Transfer to a wire rack to cool. Serve warm or cold.

CHAPTER 2

basic & everyday rolls

Bread rolls make for a quick and tasty treat any time of day; from warm, crusty rolls for breakfast to a wholesome, filling lunch or an easy teatime snack. In this chapter you will find a selection of delicious rolls, baps, knots and bagels that are ideal for everyday eating.

Try Soft Wholemeal Rolls, Floury White Baps or Malted Country Rolls – perfect for lunchboxes. For breads with added flavours, choose from Rosemary Ciabatta Rolls and Golden Cheddar Twists, or seeded breads such as Sesame Bagels and Poppyseed Knots. And for a taste of the Mediterranean, try Petits Pains au Lait, Sun-dried Tomato Rolls and Mediterranean Olive Bread Rolls.

breakfast rolls

PREPARATION TIME 15 MINUTES, PLUS MIXING & KNEADING TIME IN BREADMACHINE, PLUS RISING
COOKING TIME 15–20 MINUTES   **MAKES** 10–12 ROLLS

150ml (¼ pint / ⅔ cup) milk (at room temperature),
   plus extra for glazing
150ml (¼ pint / ⅔ cup) water
450g (1lb / 3 cups) strong plain white flour,
   plus extra for dusting

1½ tsp salt
2 tsp caster sugar
25g (1oz) butter, diced
1½ tsp fast-action dried yeast

1 Pour the milk and water into the bread pan. Sprinkle over the flour, covering the liquid completely.
   Place the salt, sugar and butter in separate corners of the pan. Make a small indent in the centre of
   the flour and add the yeast. Close the lid, set the machine to "Dough" and press Start.

2 Meanwhile, grease or flour 2 baking sheets and set aside. When the dough is ready, remove it
   from the machine, knock it back on a lightly floured surface, then divide it into 10 or 12
   equal portions.

3 Shape each portion of the into a round or oval and place on the baking sheets, spacing them well
   apart. Cover and leave to rise in a warm place for about 30 minutes, or until doubled in size.

4 Preheat the oven to 200°C/400°F/gas mark 6. Lightly brush the rolls with milk and dust with flour.
   Bake for 15–20 minutes, or until lightly browned. Transfer to a wire rack to cool. Serve warm or cold.

dinner rolls

PREPARATION TIME 15 MINUTES, PLUS MIXING & KNEADING TIME IN BREADMACHINE, PLUS RISING
COOKING TIME 15–20 MINUTES   **MAKES** 12 ROLLS

250ml (9fl oz / 1 cup) milk (at room temperature)
1 egg, beaten
450g (1lb / 3 cups) strong plain white flour
2 tsp salt
2 tsp caster sugar

55g (2oz) butter, diced
1 sachet (7g / ¼oz) fast-action dried yeast
poppy seeds or sesame seeds, for sprinkling
   (optional)

1   Pour the milk into a bowl, add the egg and whisk together. Pour the mixture into the bread pan. Sprinkle over the flour, covering the liquid completely. Add the salt, sugar and butter in separate corners of the pan. Make a small indent in the centre of the flour and add the yeast. Close the lid, set the machine to "Dough" and press Start.

2   Meanwhile, grease or flour 2 baking sheets and set aside. When the dough is ready, remove it from the machine, knock it back on a lightly floured surface, then divide it into 12 equal portions.

3   Form each portion of the dough into a round, oval or baton, or shape into a long roll or rope and tie loosely in a single knot, pulling the ends through.

4   Place the rolls on the baking sheets, spacing them well apart. Cover and leave to rise in a warm place for about 30 minutes, or until doubled in size.

5   Preheat the oven to 220°C/425°F/gas mark 7. Lightly brush the tops of the rolls with a little water and sprinkle with poppy or sesame seeds, if desired. Bake for 15–20 minutes, or until risen and golden brown. Transfer to a wire rack to cool. Serve warm or cold.

soft wholemeal rolls

PREPARATION TIME 15 MINUTES, PLUS MIXING & KNEADING TIME IN BREADMACHINE, PLUS RISING
COOKING TIME 10–15 MINUTES   **MAKES** 10–12 ROLLS

150ml (¼ pint / ⅔ cup) water
150ml (¼ pint / ⅔ cup) milk (at room temperature)
350g (12oz / 2½ cups) strong plain wholemeal flour,
    plus extra for dusting
115g (4oz / ¾ cup) strong plain white flour

1½ tsp salt
2 tsp caster sugar
25g (1oz) butter, diced
1½ tsp fast-action dried yeast

1   Pour the water and milk into the bread pan. Sprinkle over each type of flour in turn, covering the liquid completely. Add the salt, sugar and butter in separate corners of the pan. Make a small indent in the centre of the flour and add the yeast. Close the lid, set the machine to "Dough" and press Start.

2   Meanwhile, grease or flour 2 baking sheets and set aside. When the dough is ready, remove it from the machine, knock it back on a lightly floured surface, then divide it into 10 or 12 equal portions.

3   Shape each portion of the dough into a round or oval, press each one down firmly with the heel of your hand and release. Place the rolls on the baking sheets, spacing them well apart, then cover and leave to rise in a warm place for about 30 minutes, or until doubled in size.

4   Preheat the oven to 220°C/425°F/gas mark 7. Lightly dust the tops of the rolls with wholemeal flour. Bake for 10–15 minutes, or until lightly browned. Transfer to a wire rack to cool. Serve warm or cold.

floury white baps

PREPARATION TIME 15 MINUTES, PLUS MIXING & KNEADING TIME IN BREADMACHINE, PLUS RISING

COOKING TIME 15 MINUTES **MAKES** 10 BAPS

200ml (7fl oz / ¾ cup) milk (at room temperature),
    plus extra for glazing
130ml (4fl oz / ½ cup) water
450g (1lb / 3 cups) strong plain white flour,
    plus extra for dusting

1½ tsp salt
2 tsp caster sugar
1 tsp fast-action dried yeast

1   Pour the milk and water into the bread pan. Sprinkle over the flour, covering the liquid completely. Place the salt and sugar in separate corners of the pan. Make a small indent in the centre of the flour and add the yeast. Close the lid, set the machine to "Dough" and press Start.

2   Meanwhile, grease or flour 2 baking sheets and set aside. When the dough is ready, remove it from the machine, knock it back on a lightly floured surface, then divide it into 10 equal portions.

3   Shape each portion of the dough into a flat round, each about 9cm (3½in) in diameter, and place on the baking sheets, spacing them well apart. Cover and leave to rise in a warm place for about 30 minutes, or until doubled in size.

4   Preheat the oven to 200°C/400°F/gas mark 6. Gently press the centre of each bap to release any large air bubbles. Lightly brush the baps with milk and dust with flour.

5   Bake for about 15 minutes, or until lightly browned. Dust with a little more flour, then transfer to a wire rack to cool. Serve warm or cold.

scottish baps

PREPARATION TIME 15 MINUTES, PLUS MIXING & KNEADING TIME IN BREADMACHINE, PLUS RISING
COOKING TIME 15–20 MINUTES   **MAKES** 10 BAPS

150ml (¼ pint / ⅔ cup) milk (at room temperature),
    plus extra for glazing
150ml (¼ pint / ⅔ cup) water
450g (1lb / 3 cups) strong plain white flour,
    plus extra for dusting

1½ tsp salt
2 tsp caster sugar
1½ tsp fast-action dried yeast

1   Pour the milk and water into the bread pan. Sprinkle over the flour, covering the liquid completely.
    Place the salt and sugar in separate corners of the pan. Make a small indent in the centre of the flour
    and add the yeast. Close the lid, set the machine to "Dough" and press Start.

2   Meanwhile, grease or flour 2 baking sheets and set aside. When the dough is ready, remove it from
    the machine, knock it back on a lightly floured surface, then divide it into 10 equal portions.

3   Roll or pat each portion of the dough into a round or oval about 1cm (½in) thick. Place on the baking
    sheets, spacing them well apart, then cover and leave to rise in a warm place for about 30 minutes,
    or until doubled in size.

4   Preheat the oven to 200°C/400°F/gas mark 6. Gently press the centre of each bap to release any
    large air bubbles. Lightly brush the baps with milk and dust with flour.

5   Bake for 15–20 minutes, or until lightly browned. Dust the tops with a little more flour, then transfer
    to a wire rack to cool. Serve warm.

rosemary ciabatta rolls

PREPARATION TIME 20 MINUTES, PLUS MIXING & KNEADING TIME IN BREADMACHINE, PLUS RISING
COOKING TIME 20 MINUTES   **MAKES** ABOUT 10 GOOD-SIZED ROLLS

350ml (12fl oz / 1⅓ cups) water
2 tbsp olive oil
500g (1lb 2oz / 3½ cups) strong plain white flour,
    plus extra for dusting
1 tsp salt

1 tsp granulated sugar
1 tsp fast-action dried yeast
1 tbsp finely chopped fresh rosemary
milk, for glazing

1   Pour the water into the bread pan, then add the oil. Sprinkle over the flour, covering the liquid
    completely. Place the salt and sugar in separate corners of the pan. Make a small indent in the centre
    of the flour and add the yeast. Close the lid, set the machine to "Dough" and press Start.

2   Meanwhile, grease or flour 2 baking sheets and set aside. When the dough is ready, remove it from
    the machine, knock it back on a lightly floured surface, then knead the chopped rosemary evenly into
    the dough.

3   Divide the dough into about 10 equal portions. Roll and shape each portion into a round or oval, then
    flatten them slightly. Place on the baking sheets, spacing them well apart. Cover and leave to rise in a
    warm place for about 30 minutes, or until doubled in size.

4   Preheat the oven to 200°C/400°F/gas mark 6. Brush the tops of the rolls with milk and dust with flour.

5   Bake for about 20 minutes, or until the rolls are golden brown and sound hollow when tapped
    underneath. Transfer to a wire rack to cool. Serve warm.

panini rolls

PREPARATION TIME 15 MINUTES, PLUS MIXING & KNEADING TIME IN BREADMACHINE, PLUS RISING
COOKING TIME 15 MINUTES   **MAKES** 12 ROLLS

265ml (9½ fl oz / 1 cup) water
4 tbsp extra-virgin olive oil, plus extra for glazing
450g (1lb / 3 cups) strong plain white flour

2 tsp salt
2 tsp caster sugar
1 sachet (7g / ¼ oz) fast-action dried yeast

1   Pour the water into the bread pan, then add the oil. Sprinkle over the flour, covering the liquid completely. Place the salt and sugar in separate corners of the pan. Make a small indent in the centre of the flour and add the yeast. Close the lid, set the machine to "Dough" and press Start.

2   Meanwhile, grease or flour 2 baking sheets and set aside. When the dough is ready, remove it from the machine, knock it back on a lightly floured surface, then divide it into 12 equal portions.

3   Shape each portion of the dough into a ball and place on the baking sheets, spacing them well apart. Brush with olive oil, cover and leave to rise in a warm place for 20–30 minutes, or until doubled in size.

4   Preheat the oven to 200°C/400°F/gas mark 6. Using a sharp knife, cut a cross in the top of each roll. Bake for about 15 minutes, or until golden brown. Transfer to a wire rack to cool. Serve warm or cold.

malted country rolls

PREPARATION TIME 15 MINUTES, PLUS MIXING & KNEADING TIME IN BREADMACHINE, PLUS RISING
COOKING TIME 15–20 MINUTES   **MAKES** 10–12 ROLLS

150ml (¼ pint / ⅔ cup) milk (at room temperature),
    plus extra for glazing
125ml (4fl oz / ½ cup) water
1 tbsp malt extract
450g (1lb / 3¼ cups) strong malted Granary flour

2 tsp salt
2 tsp soft light brown sugar
25g (1oz) butter, diced
1½ tsp fast-action dried yeast
kibbled or cracked wheat, for sprinkling

1   Pour the milk and water into the bread pan, then add the malt extract. Sprinkle over the flour,
    covering the liquid completely. Place the salt, sugar and butter in separate corners of the pan.
    Make a small indent in the centre of the flour and add the yeast. Close the lid, set the machine to
    "Dough" and press Start.

2   Meanwhile, grease or flour 2 baking sheets and set aside. When the dough is ready, remove it from
    the machine, knock it back on a lightly floured surface, then divide it into 10 or 12 equal portions.

3   Shape each portion of the into a round or oval and place on the baking sheets, spacing them well
    apart. Gently press down on each roll to flatten slightly. Cover and leave to rise in a warm place until
    doubled in size.

4   Preheat the oven to 200°C/400°F/gas mark 6. Lightly brush the rolls with milk and sprinkle with
    kibbled or cracked wheat. Bake for 15–20 minutes, or until lightly browned. Transfer to a wire rack to
    cool. Serve warm or cold.

golden cheddar twists

PREPARATION TIME 20 MINUTES, PLUS MIXING & KNEADING TIME IN BREADMACHINE, PLUS RISING
COOKING TIME 15–20 MINUTES   **MAKES** 10 TWISTS

325ml (11fl oz / 1⅓ cups) warm water (or according
    to bread-mix packet instructions)
500g (1lb 2oz) packet white bread mix
1 tsp mustard powder

a few turns of freshly ground black pepper
115g (4oz / scant 1 cup) mature Cheddar cheese,
    finely grated
beaten egg or milk, for glazing

1   Pour the correct amount of water into the bread pan. Sprinkle over the bread mix, covering the water
    completely. Sprinkle over the mustard powder and black pepper, then sprinkle over 85g (3oz / ¾ cup)
    of the cheese. Close the lid, set the machine to "Dough" and press Start.

2   Grease or flour 2 baking sheets and set aside. When the dough is ready, remove it from the machine,
    knock it back on a lightly floured surface, then divide it into 10 equal portions.

3   Roll each portion of the into a long sausage or rope shape and gently tie each one loosely in a single
    knot. Place on the baking sheets, spacing them well apart, brush with beaten egg or milk and sprinkle
    with the remaining cheese. Cover and leave to rise in a warm place until doubled in size.

4   Preheat the oven to 200°C/400°F/gas mark 6. Bake the rolls for 15–20 minutes, or until risen and
    golden brown. Transfer to a wire rack to cool. Serve warm or cold.

sun-dried tomato rolls

PREPARATION TIME 20 MINUTES, PLUS MIXING & KNEADING TIME IN BREADMACHINE, PLUS RISING
COOKING TIME 20 MINUTES   **MAKES** ABOUT 10 GOOD-SIZED ROLLS

350ml (12fl oz / 1⅓ cups) water
2 tbsp oil from a jar of sun-dried tomatoes
500g (1lb 2oz / 3½ cups) strong plain white flour,
    plus extra for dusting
1 tsp salt

1 tsp granulated sugar
1 tsp fast-action dried yeast
115g (4oz / 1 cup) sun-dried tomatoes in oil
    (drained weight), patted dry and chopped
milk, for glazing

1   Pour the water into the bread pan, then add the oil. Sprinkle over the flour, covering the liquid completely. Place the salt and sugar in separate corners of the pan. Make a small indent in the centre of the flour and add the yeast. Close the lid, set the machine to "Dough" and press Start.

2   Meanwhile, grease or flour 2 baking sheets and set aside. When the dough is ready, remove it from the machine, knock it back on a lightly floured surface, then knead the chopped tomatoes evenly into the dough.

3   Divide the dough into about 10 equal portions. Roll and shape each portion into a round or oval, then flatten slightly. Place on the baking sheets, spacing them well apart. Cover and leave to rise in a warm place for about 30 minutes, or until doubled in size.

4   Preheat the oven to 200°C/400°F/gas mark 6. Brush the tops of the rolls with milk and dust with flour. Bake for about 20 minutes, or until the rolls are golden brown and sound hollow when tapped underneath. Transfer to a wire rack to cool. Serve warm.

mediterranean olive bread rolls

PREPARATION TIME 20 MINUTES, PLUS MIXING & KNEADING TIME IN BREADMACHINE, PLUS RISING
COOKING TIME 20 MINUTES **MAKES** ABOUT 10 GOOD-SIZED ROLLS

350ml (12fl oz / 1⅓ cups) water
2 tbsp extra-virgin olive oil, plus extra for glazing
500g (1lb 2oz / 3½ cups) strong plain white flour
1 tsp salt

1 tsp granulated sugar
1 tsp fast-action dried yeast
115g (4oz / ¾ cup) pitted black olives
   (drained weight), chopped

1   Pour the water into the bread pan, then add the oil. Sprinkle over the flour, covering the liquid completely. Place the salt and sugar in separate corners of the pan. Make a small indent in the centre of the flour and add the yeast. Close the lid, set the machine to "Dough" and press Start.

2   Meanwhile, grease or flour 2 baking sheets and set aside. When the dough is ready, remove it from the machine, knock it back on a lightly floured surface, then knead the chopped olives evenly into the dough. Divide the dough into about 10 equal portions.

3   Roll and shape each portion of the into a round or oval, then flatten slightly. Place on the baking sheets, spacing them well apart. Cover and leave to rise in a warm place for about 30 minutes, or until doubled in size.

4   Preheat the oven to 200°C/400°F/gas mark 6. Brush the tops of the rolls with olive oil. Bake for about 20 minutes, or until the rolls are golden brown and sound hollow when tapped underneath. Transfer to a wire rack to cool. Serve warm.

Variation Knead 1–2 tablespoons chopped fresh mixed herbs into the dough with the olives, if desired.

petits pains au lait

PREPARATION TIME 15 MINUTES, PLUS MIXING & KNEADING TIME IN BREADMACHINE, PLUS RISING
COOKING TIME 15–20 MINUTES   **MAKES** 12 ROLLS

300ml (½ pint / 1¼ cups) milk (at room temperature),
    plus extra for glazing
450g (1lb / 3 cups) strong plain white flour
1½ tsp salt

1 tbsp caster sugar
55g (2oz) butter, diced
2 tsp fast-action dried yeast

1   Pour the milk into the bread pan. Sprinkle over the flour, covering the milk completely. Place the salt, sugar and butter in separate corners of the pan. Make a small indent in the centre of the flour and add the yeast. Close the lid, set the machine to "Dough" and press Start.

2   Meanwhile, grease or flour 2 baking sheets and set aside. When the dough is ready, remove it from the machine, knock it back on a lightly floured surface, then divide it into 12 equal portions.

3   Shape each portion of the dough into a 13cm (5in) long roll, tapered at each end, and place on the baking sheets, spacing them well apart. Cover and leave to rise in a warm place for 20–30 minutes, or until doubled in size.

4   Preheat the oven to 200°C/400°F/gas mark 6. Using a sharp knife, slash the top of each roll diagonally several times at regular intervals, then brush them with milk.

5   Bake for 15–20 minutes, or until golden brown. Transfer to a wire rack to cool. Serve warm or cold.

sesame bagels

PREPARATION TIME 10 MINUTES, PLUS MIXING & KNEADING TIME IN BREADMACHINE, PLUS 10 MINUTES TO SHAPE BAGELS, PLUS RISING **COOKING TIME** 30–35 MINUTES   **MAKES** 12 BAGELS

275ml (9½fl oz / 1 cup) water
2 tbsp sunflower oil
450g (1lb / 3 cups) strong plain white flour
1½ tsp salt
1 tbsp caster sugar

1 sachet (7g / ¼oz) fast-action dried yeast
1 tbsp malt extract
milk or water, for glazing
about 2 tbsp sesame seeds, for sprinkling

1 Pour the water into the bread pan, then add the oil. Sprinkle over the flour, covering the liquid completely. Place the salt and sugar in separate corners of the pan. Make a small indent in the centre of the flour and add the yeast. Close the lid, set the machine to "Dough" and press Start.

2 Meanwhile, grease 2 baking sheets and set aside. When the dough is ready, remove it from the machine, knock it back on a lightly floured surface, then divide it into 12 equal portions.

3 Shape each portion of the dough into a ball, then, using a floured wooden spoon handle, make a hole through the centre of each ball. Enlarge the holes by pulling the dough outwards a little to form rings (bear in mind that the holes will close slightly when the dough is risen and poached). Place on the baking sheets, cover and leave to rise in a warm place until doubled in size.

4 Preheat the oven to 200°C/400°F/gas mark 6. Heat a large pan of water to simmering, then stir in the malt extract. Drop each bagel into the water (three or four at a time) and poach for about 3 minutes, turning once. Remove from the water, drain well, then return the bagels to the baking sheets.

5 Brush each bagel with a little milk or water and sprinkle the tops with sesame seeds. Bake for about 20 minutes, or until cooked and golden brown. Transfer to a wire rack to cool. Cut in half to serve.

poppyseed knots (pictured left)

PREPARATION TIME 20 MINUTES, PLUS MIXING & KNEADING TIME IN BREADMACHINE, PLUS RISING
COOKING TIME 15–20 MINUTES   **MAKES** 10 KNOTS

325ml (11fl oz / 1⅓ cups) warm water (or according
    to bread-mix packet instructions)
500g (1lb 2oz) packet white bread mix

beaten egg or milk, for glazing
poppy seeds, for sprinkling

1   Pour the correct amount of water into the bread pan. Sprinkle over the bread mix, covering the water completely. Close the lid, set the machine to "Dough" and press Start.

2   Meanwhile, grease or flour 2 baking sheets and set aside. When the dough is ready, remove it from the machine, knock it back on a lightly floured surface, then divide it into 10 equal portions.

3   Roll each portion of the dough into a long sausage or rope shape and gently tie each one loosely in a single knot. Place on the baking sheets, spacing them well apart, then brush with beaten egg or milk and sprinkle with poppy seeds. Cover and leave to rise in a warm place until doubled in size.

4   Preheat the oven to 200°C/400°F/gas mark 6. Bake the rolls for 15–20 minutes, or until risen and golden brown. Transfer to a wire rack to cool. Serve warm or cold.

seeded knots

PREPARATION TIME 20 MINUTES, PLUS MIXING & KNEADING TIME IN BREADMACHINE, PLUS RISING
COOKING TIME 15–20 MINUTES   **MAKES** 12 KNOTS

340ml (11½fl oz / 1⅓ cups) milk (at room temperature)
500g (1lb 2oz / 3½ cups) strong plain white flour
2 tsp salt
2 tsp caster sugar

25g (1oz) butter, diced
1 sachet (7g / ¼oz) fast-action dried yeast
caraway seeds, pumpkin seeds and poppy seeds,
    for sprinkling

1   Pour the milk into the bread pan. Sprinkle over the flour, covering the milk completely. Place the salt, sugar and butter in separate corners of the pan. Make a small indent in the centre of the flour and add the yeast. Close the lid, set the machine to "Dough" and press Start.

2   Meanwhile, grease or flour 2 baking sheets and set aside. When the dough is ready, remove it from the machine, knock it back on a lightly floured surface, then divide it into 12 equal portions.

3   Roll each portion of the into a long sausage or rope shape and gently tie each one loosely in a single knot. Place on the baking sheets, spacing them well apart, then cover and leave to rise in a warm place for about 30 minutes, or until doubled in size.

4   Preheat the oven to 220°C/425°F/gas mark 7. Lightly brush the rolls with a little water and sprinkle 4 rolls with caraway seeds, 4 with pumpkin seeds and 4 with poppy seeds. Bake for 15–20 minutes, or until risen and golden brown. Transfer to a wire rack to cool. Serve warm or cold.

CHAPTER 3

flat breads

Flat breads, whether leavened or unleavened, vary in texture, flavour and shape. They may be crisp or chewy, plain or rich, and most of them are quick and easy to prepare and cook.

Many flat breads provide an ideal accompaniment to numerous dishes; some are great for dipping or mopping up sauces, while others are perfect for filling or wrapping to create a quick supper or snack.

We include a whole variety of tempting flat bread recipes from around the world, ranging from flavourful Spiced Naan Breads and North African Flat Breads to Sun-dried Tomato & Olive Focaccia and Pancetta, Pepper & Olive Pizzas.

pitta breads

PREPARATION TIME 15 MINUTES, PLUS MIXING & KNEADING TIME IN BREADMACHINE, PLUS RISING
COOKING TIME 10 MINUTES   **MAKES** 8 PITTA BREADS

225ml (8fl oz / ¾ cup) water
1 tbsp olive oil
350g (12oz / 2½ cups) strong plain white flour

1½ tsp salt
1 tsp caster sugar
1 tsp fast-action dried yeast

1   Pour the water into the bread pan, then add the oil. Sprinkle over the flour, covering the liquid completely. Place the salt and sugar in separate corners of the pan. Make a small indent in the centre of the flour and add the yeast. Close the lid, set the machine to "Basic Dough" or "Pizza Dough" and press Start.

2   When the dough is ready, remove it from the machine, knock it back on a lightly floured surface, then divide it into 8 equal portions.

3   Roll out each portion of the dough to form a flat oval, about 3–5mm (⅛–¼in) thick and about 14–15cm (5½–6in) in length. Lay the dough ovals on a floured tea towel, cover and leave to rise at normal room temperature for about 30 minutes.

4   Preheat the oven to 230°C/450°F/gas mark 8. Put 3 baking sheets in the oven to heat. Place the pitta breads on the hot baking sheets and bake for about 10 minutes, or until puffed up and golden brown.

5   Serve warm or wrap in a clean tea towel and leave to cool on a wire rack, then re-heat under a grill when required. To serve, split open and stuff with your favourite filling.

focaccia breads

PREPARATION TIME 15 MINUTES, PLUS MIXING & KNEADING TIME IN BREADMACHINE, PLUS RISING
COOKING TIME 20–25 MINUTES   **MAKES** 8 FOCACCIA BREADS

240ml (8½fl oz / 1 cup) water
3 tbsp olive oil, plus extra for drizzling
450g (1lb / 3 cups) strong plain white flour
1 tsp salt

1½ tsp granulated sugar
1½ tsp fast-action dried yeast
coarse sea salt, for sprinkling

1   Pour the water into the bread pan, then add the oil. Sprinkle over the flour, covering the liquid
    completely. Place the salt and sugar in separate corners of the pan. Make a small indent in the centre
    of the flour and add the yeast. Close the lid, set the machine to "Basic Dough" or "Pizza Dough" and
    press Start.
2   Meanwhile, grease or flour 2 baking sheets and set aside. When the dough is ready, remove it from
    the machine, knock it back on a lightly floured surface, then divide it into 8 equal portions.
3   Roll each portion of the dough into a ball, then flatten each ball into a round about 10cm (4in) in
    diameter, making the edges slightly thicker than the centres. Place on the baking sheets, cover and
    leave to rise in a warm place for about 30–45 minutes, or until slightly risen.
4   Preheat the oven to 200°C/400°F/gas mark 6. Drizzle a little olive oil over each focaccia, sprinkle with
    sea salt and spray with a little water.
5   Bake for 20–25 minutes, or until risen and golden brown, spraying with a little water again after
    the first 5 minutes of cooking. Transfer to a wire rack to cool. Serve warm or cold, whole or cut
    into quarters.

sun-dried tomato & olive focaccia

PREPARATION TIME 20 MINUTES, PLUS MIXING & KNEADING TIME IN BREADMACHINE, PLUS RISING

COOKING TIME 20–25 MINUTES   **MAKES** 1 LOAF (SERVES 6–8)

300ml (½ pint / 1¼ cups) water
3 tbsp olive oil, plus extra for drizzling
500g (1lb 2oz / 3½ cups) strong plain white flour
1 tsp salt
1 tsp granulated sugar
1 tsp fast-action dried yeast

55g (2oz / ½ cup) sun-dried tomatoes in oil
    (drained weight), patted dry and chopped
55g (2oz / ⅓ cup) pitted black olives
    (drained weight), chopped
coarse sea salt, for sprinkling

1   Pour the water into the bread pan, then add the oil. Sprinkle over the flour, covering the liquid completely. Place the salt and sugar in separate corners of the pan. Make a small indent in the centre of the flour and add the yeast. Close the lid, set the machine to "Basic Raisin Dough" (or equivalent), or "Dough", and press Start.

2   Add the tomatoes and olives when the machine makes a sound (beeps) to add extra ingredients during the kneading cycle (or add 5 minutes before the end of the kneading cycle).

3   Meanwhile, grease or flour a baking sheet and set aside. When the dough is ready, remove it from the machine, knock it back on a lightly floured surface, then roll out the dough to form a large, flat oval about 2.5cm (1in) thick. Place on the baking sheet, cover and leave to rise in a warm place until doubled in size.

4   Preheat the oven to 200°C/400°F/gas mark 6. Using your fingertips, make deep dimples all over the surface of the dough. Drizzle with oil and sprinkle with sea salt.

5   Bake for 20–25 minutes, or until cooked and golden. Transfer to a wire rack to cool. Serve warm or cold in chunks or slices.

north african flat breads

PREPARATION TIME 10 MINUTES, PLUS MIXING & KNEADING TIME IN BREADMACHINE, PLUS RISING
COOKING TIME 15–20 MINUTES   **MAKES** 8 FLAT BREADS

225ml (8fl oz / ¾ cup) water
5 tbsp olive oil, plus extra for glazing
500g (1lb 2oz / 3½ cups) strong plain white flour,
    plus extra for dusting

2 tsp salt
1½ tsp caster sugar
1½ tsp fast-action dried yeast

1   Pour the water into the bread pan, then add the oil. Sprinkle over the flour, covering the liquid completely. Place the salt and sugar in separate corners of the pan. Make a small indent in the centre of the flour and add the yeast. Close the lid, set the machine to "Basic Dough" or "Pizza Dough" and press Start.

2   Meanwhile, grease or flour 2 baking sheets and set aside. When the dough is ready, remove it from the machine, knock it back on a lightly floured surface, then divide it into 8 equal portions.

3   Roll out each portion of the to make a flat round about 10cm (4in) in diameter. Place on the baking sheets, then cover and leave to rise in a warm place for about 1 hour, or until slightly risen.

4   Preheat the oven to 230°C/450°F/gas mark 8. Brush a little oil over the top of each flat bread and dust with a little flour. Bake for 15–20 minutes, or until risen and golden brown. Serve warm.

moroccan flat breads

PREPARATION TIME 15 MINUTES, PLUS MIXING & KNEADING TIME IN BREADMACHINE, PLUS RESTING
COOKING TIME 15–20 MINUTES   **MAKES** 4 FLAT BREADS

175ml (6fl oz / ⅔ cup) milk (at room temperature)
280g (10oz / 2 cups) strong plain white flour
1 tsp fennel seeds
1 tsp salt

2 tsp clear honey
1 tsp fast-action dried yeast
beaten egg, for glazing

1   Pour the milk into the bread pan. Sprinkle over the flour, covering the milk completely, then sprinkle over the fennel seeds. Place the salt and honey in separate corners of the pan. Make a small indent in the centre of the flour and add the yeast. Close the lid, set the machine to "Basic Dough" or "Pizza Dough" and press Start.

2   Grease or flour 2 baking sheets and set aside. When the dough is ready, remove it from the machine, knock it back on a lightly floured surface, then divide it into 4 equal portions.

3   Roll the dough into rounds about 9cm (3½in) in diameter, and about 2cm (¾in) thick. Place on the baking sheets, then, using a sharp knife or scissors, cut twelve 1cm (½in) deep slashes all around the edge of each dough round at regular intervals. Cover and leave in a warm place for 20 minutes.

4   Preheat the oven to 220°C/425°F/gas mark 7. Brush the tops of the dough rounds with beaten egg, then bake for 15–20 minutes, or until the breads are risen slightly and golden brown. Transfer to a wire rack to cool. Serve whole or cut into quarters.

pancetta, pepper & olive pizzas

PREPARATION TIME 30 MINUTES, PLUS MIXING & KNEADING TIME IN BREADMACHINE
COOKING TIME 20–25 MINUTES   **MAKES** 2 PIZZAS (EACH PIZZA SERVES 4–6)

FOR THE PIZZA DOUGH
280ml (9½fl oz / 1 cup) water
2 tbsp olive oil
450g (1lb / 3 cups) strong plain white flour
1 tsp salt
2 tsp caster sugar
1½ tsp fast-action dried yeast

FOR THE TOPPING
2 tbsp olive oil
2 cloves garlic, crushed
225g (8oz / 1 cup) smoked pancetta, diced
2 large red peppers, seeded and sliced
400g (14oz) can chopped tomatoes with herbs,
    drained
2 tbsp tomato purée
sea salt and freshly ground black pepper
115–175g (4–6oz / ¾–1 heaped cup) pitted
    black olives
115g (4oz / ¾ cup) Parmesan cheese, grated
basil leaves (optional)

1   Make the dough. Pour the water into the bread pan, then add the oil. Sprinkle over the flour, covering
    the liquid completely. Place the salt and sugar in separate corners of the pan. Make a small indent
    in the centre of the flour and add the yeast. Close the lid, set the machine to "Basic Dough" or "Pizza
    Dough" and press Start.

2   Meanwhile, grease or flour 2 baking sheets and set aside.

3   Prepare the topping. Heat the oil in a frying pan, add the garlic and sauté for 30 seconds. Add the
    pancetta and stir-fry over a high heat until it releases its fat and browns lightly. Remove from the pan
    and set aside. Add the peppers to the pan and sauté until just softened. Remove the pan from the
    heat and add the pancetta to the peppers.

4   When the dough is ready, remove it from the machine, knock it back on a lightly floured surface, then
    divide it in half. Roll out each piece of dough thinly to form a 30cm (12in) round. Transfer each round
    to a baking sheet.

5   Preheat the oven to 220°C/425°F/gas mark 7. Mix together the tomatoes, tomato purée and
    seasoning. Spread this mixture evenly over the pizza bases to within 1cm (½in) of the edge. Spoon
    the pepper and pancetta mixture evenly over the tomatoes, then scatter the olives over the top.
    Sprinkle with the Parmesan cheese.

6   Bake for 20–25 minutes, or until the base is crisp and the topping is golden. Serve warm, sprinkled
    with basil leaves, if using.

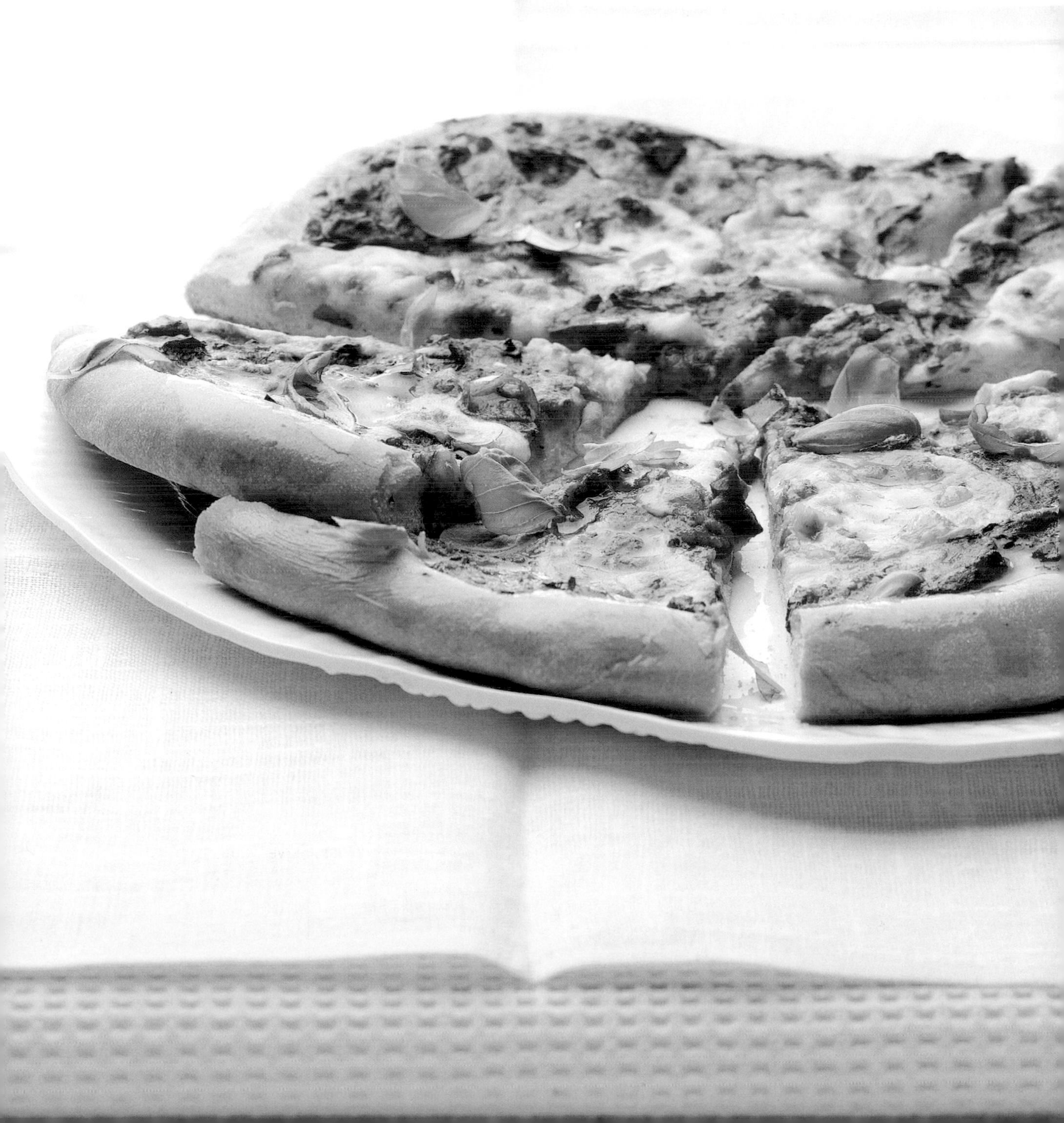

naan breads

PREPARATION TIME 10 MINUTES, PLUS MIXING & KNEADING TIME IN BREADMACHINE, PLUS RESTING
COOKING TIME 10–12 MINUTES   **MAKES** 4 GOOD-SIZED NAAN BREADS

120ml (4fl oz / ½ cup) milk (at room temperature)
4 tbsp natural yogurt (at room temperature)
1 tbsp sunflower oil
300g (10½oz / 2 cups) strong plain white flour

1 tsp salt
1½ tsp caster sugar
1 tsp fast-action dried yeast
about 3 tbsp melted ghee or butter, for brushing

1   Pour the milk into a bowl, add the yogurt and oil and whisk well. Pour the mixture into the bread pan. Sprinkle over the flour, covering the liquid completely. Place the salt and sugar in separate corners of the pan. Make a small indent in the centre of the flour and add the yeast. Close the lid, set the machine to "Basic Dough" or "Pizza Dough" and press Start.

2   When the dough is ready, remove it from the machine, knock it back on a lightly floured surface, then divide it into 4 equal portions.

3   Roll out each portion of the to form a flat oval or teardrop shape, about 5mm (¼in) thick and 23cm (9in) long. Cover and leave for 15 minutes.

4   Preheat the oven to 230°C/450°F/gas mark 8. Put 2 baking sheets in the oven to heat. Place the naan breads on the hot baking sheets and brush with melted ghee or butter. Bake for 10–12 minutes, or until puffed up. Wrap in a clean tea towel and serve warm.

spiced naan breads

PREPARATION TIME 10 MINUTES, PLUS MIXING & KNEADING TIME IN BREADMACHINE, PLUS RESTING

COOKING TIME 10–12 MINUTES   **MAKES** 4 GOOD-SIZED NAAN BREADS

120ml (4fl oz / ½ cup) milk (at room temperature)
4 tbsp natural yogurt (at room temperature)
1 tbsp sunflower oil
300g (10½oz / 2 cups) strong plain white flour
1½ tsp ground coriander
1 tsp ground cumin

1 tsp hot chilli powder
1 tsp salt
1½ tsp caster sugar
1 tsp fast-action dried yeast
about 3 tbsp melted ghee or butter, for brushing

1   Pour the milk into a bowl, add the yogurt and oil and whisk well. Pour the mixture into the bread pan. Sprinkle over the flour, covering the liquid completely. Mix the ground spices together, then sprinkle the spices over the flour. Place the salt and sugar in separate corners of the pan. Make a small indent in the centre of the flour and add the yeast. Close the lid, set the machine to "Basic Dough" or "Pizza Dough" and press Start.

2   When the dough is ready, remove it from the machine, knock it back on a lightly floured surface, then divide it into 4 equal portions.

3   Roll out each portion of the to form a flat oval or teardrop shape, about 5mm (¼in) thick and 23cm (9in) long. Cover and leave for 15 minutes.

4   Preheat the oven to 230°C/450°F/gas mark 8. Put 2 baking sheets in the oven to heat. Place the naan breads on the hot baking sheets and brush with melted ghee or butter. Bake for 10–12 minutes, or until puffed up. Wrap in a clean tea towel and serve warm.

garlic & coriander naan breads

PREPARATION TIME 10 MINUTES, PLUS MIXING & KNEADING TIME IN BREADMACHINE, PLUS RESTING
COOKING TIME 10–12 MINUTES   **MAKES** 4 GOOD-SIZED NAAN BREADS

120ml (4fl oz / ½ cup) milk (at room temperature)
4 tbsp natural yogurt (at room temperature)
1 tbsp sunflower oil
300g (10½oz / 2 cups) strong plain white flour
1½ tsp ground coriander
1 large clove garlic, crushed

1 tsp salt
1½ tsp caster sugar
1 tsp fast-action dried yeast
about 3 tbsp melted ghee or butter, for brushing
1–2 tsp black onion seeds
1–2 tbsp chopped fresh coriander

1   Pour the milk into a bowl, add the yogurt and oil and whisk well. Pour the mixture into the bread pan. Sprinkle over the flour, covering the liquid completely. Sprinkle the ground coriander and garlic over the flour. Place the salt and sugar in separate corners of the pan. Make a small indent in the centre of the flour and add the yeast. Close the lid, set the machine to "Basic Dough" or "Pizza Dough" and press Start.

2   When the dough is ready, remove it from the machine, knock it back on a lightly floured surface, then divide it into 4 equal portions.

3   Roll out each portion of the to form a flat oval or teardrop shape, about 5mm (¼in) thick and 23cm (9in) long. Cover and leave for 15 minutes.

4   Preheat the oven to 230°C/450°F/gas mark 8. Put 2 baking sheets in the oven to heat. Place the naan breads on the hot baking sheets, brush with melted ghee or butter, then sprinkle with onion seeds and chopped fresh coriander. Bake for 10–12 minutes, or until puffed up. Wrap in a clean tea towel and serve warm.

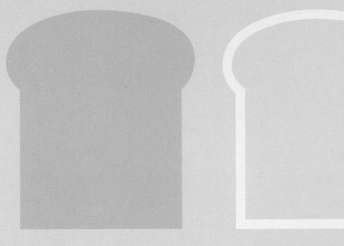

CHAPTER 4

quick breads

Quick breads are quick and easy to make compared to many other types of bread: ingredients are simply mixed together and baked, without the need for prolonged kneading or rising periods, creating a range of delicious sweet and savoury breads.

Some quick breads, such as those that have been enriched with butter, eggs or dried fruit, should keep well for several days if wrapped in foil or stored in an airtight container. Others are best served freshly baked and warm from the oven.

We include a wide range of versatile and tasty quick breads to tempt you. Choose from traditional favourites such Golden Gingerbread and Malted Fruit Loaf, or experiment with different flavour combinations such as Cheese & Date Bread or Celery & Walnut Loaf.

golden gingerbread

PREPARATION TIME 20 MINUTES, PLUS COOLING   **COOKING TIME** 1 HOUR–1 HOUR 10 MINUTES
MAKES 1 LOAF (SERVES 8–10)

115g (4oz / ⅔ cup packed) soft light brown sugar
85g (3oz) butter
175g (6oz / ½ cup) golden syrup
225g (8oz / 1⅔ cups) plain white flour
a pinch of salt

1 tsp baking powder
2 tsp ground ginger
1 egg, beaten
150ml (¼ pint / ⅔ cup) milk

1   Remove the kneading blade from the bread pan. Remove the bread pan from the machine, grease and line the base and sides of the pan and set aside.

2   Place the sugar, butter and syrup in a small saucepan and heat gently, stirring, until melted and blended. Remove from the heat and cool slightly. Sift the flour, salt, baking powder and ginger into a bowl and make a well in the centre. Mix together the egg and milk and pour into the well along with the melted mixture. Beat together using a wooden spoon until smooth and thoroughly mixed. Pour the mixture into the bread pan.

3   Place the bread pan in position in the machine and close the lid. Set the machine to "Bake Only" for 60 minutes. Press Start.

4   After baking, a fine skewer inserted in the centre of the gingerbread should come out clean. If the gingerbread requires further baking, bake on the same setting for a further 5–10 minutes, or until cooked.

5   Remove the bread pan from the machine using oven gloves, then leave to stand for 5 minutes, before turning the gingerbread out onto a wire rack to cool. Serve warm or cold in slices.

date & walnut loaf

PREPARATION TIME 20 MINUTES, PLUS 15 MINUTES STANDING   **COOKING TIME** 45–55 MINUTES

MAKES 1 LOAF (SERVES 10–12)

225g (8oz / 1¼ cups) pitted dried dates, chopped
150ml (¼ pint / ⅔ cup) boiling water
85g (3oz) butter, softened
85g (3oz / ½ cup packed) soft light brown sugar

1 egg, beaten
225g (8oz / 1⅓ cups) self-raising white flour
1 tsp baking powder
85g (3oz / ⅔ cup) walnuts, chopped

1   Remove the kneading blade from the bread pan. Remove the bread pan from the machine, grease and line the base and sides of the pan and set aside.

2   Place the dates in a bowl and pour over the boiling water. Stir to mix, then set aside for 15 minutes. Cream the butter and sugar together in a separate bowl until pale and fluffy, then gradually beat in the egg. Fold in the flour, baking powder, walnuts and date mixture, stirring until well mixed. Spoon the mixture into the bread pan and level the surface.

3   Place the bread pan in position in the machine and close the lid. Set the machine to "Bake Only" for 45 minutes. Press Start.

4   After baking, a fine skewer inserted in the centre of the loaf should come out clean. If the loaf requires further baking, bake on the same setting for a further 5–10 minutes, or until cooked.

5   Remove the bread pan from the machine using oven gloves, then leave to stand for 5 minutes, before turning the loaf out onto a wire rack to cool. Serve warm or cold in slices.

cheese & date bread

PREPARATION TIME 20 MINUTES   **COOKING TIME** 45–55 MINUTES   **MAKES** 1 LOAF (SERVES 8–10)

225g (8oz / 1⅔ cups) self-raising white flour
a pinch of salt
55g (2oz) butter, diced
85g (3oz / ⅔ cup) mature Cheddar cheese, finely grated

115g (4oz / ⅔ cup) pitted dried dates, finely chopped
2 eggs
150ml (¼ pint / ⅔ cup) milk

1   Remove the kneading blade from the bread pan. Remove the bread pan from the machine, grease and line the base and sides of the pan and set aside.

2   Sift the flour and salt into a bowl, then lightly rub in the butter until the mixture resembles breadcrumbs. Stir in 70g (2½oz / scant ⅔ cup) of the cheese and the dates. Beat the eggs and milk together in a separate bowl, then add to the date mixture and mix well to combine. Spoon the mixture into the bread pan and level the surface. Sprinkle with the remaining cheese.

3   Place the bread pan in position in the machine and close the lid. Set the machine to "Bake Only" for 45 minutes. Press Start.

4   After baking, a fine skewer inserted in the centre of the loaf should come out clean. If the loaf requires further baking, bake on the same setting for a further 5–10 minutes, or until cooked.

5   Remove the bread pan from the machine using oven gloves, then leave to stand for 5 minutes, before turning the loaf out onto a wire rack to cool. Serve warm or cold in slices.

fruity hazelnut loaf

PREPARATION TIME 20 MINUTES, PLUS 30 MINUTES SOAKING   **COOKING TIME** 1 HOUR–1 HOUR 10 MINUTES
MAKES 1 LOAF (SERVES 10–12)

85g (3oz / ½ cup) sultanas
85g (3oz / ½ cup) ready-to-eat dried apricots,
   roughly chopped
85g (3oz / 1⅓ cups) bran
300ml (½ pint / 1¼ cups) milk
115g (4oz / ¾ cup) self-raising white flour
a pinch of salt

115g (4oz / ¾ cup) self-raising wholemeal flour
55g (2oz) butter, diced
115g (4oz / scant 1 cup) hazelnuts, chopped
115g (4oz / ¾ cup) demerara sugar
1 tsp ground mixed spice
2 eggs, beaten

1 Place the sultanas, apricots and bran in a bowl, add the milk and mix well. Cover and leave to soak for 30 minutes. Remove the kneading blade from the bread pan, remove the bread pan from the machine, grease and line the base and sides of the pan and set aside.

2 Sift the white flour and salt into a bowl, stir in the wholemeal flour, then lightly rub in the butter until the mixture resembles breadcrumbs. Add the bran mixture, hazelnuts, sugar, mixed spice and eggs and mix thoroughly. Spoon the mixture into the bread pan and level the surface.

3 Place the bread pan in position in the machine and close the lid. Set the machine to "Bake Only" for 60 minutes. Press Start.

4 After baking, a fine skewer inserted in the centre of the loaf should come out clean. If the loaf requires further baking, bake on the same setting for a further 5–10 minutes, or until cooked.

5 Remove the bread pan from the machine using oven gloves, then leave to stand for 5 minutes, before turning the loaf out onto a wire rack to cool. Serve warm or cold in slices.

banana & honey loaf

PREPARATION TIME 20 MINUTES   **COOKING TIME** 1 HOUR–1 HOUR 10 MINUTES

MAKES 1 LOAF (SERVES 8–10)

115g (4oz) butter, softened
115g (4oz / ⅔ cup packed) soft light brown sugar
115g (4oz / ⅓ cup) thick (set) honey
2 eggs, beaten

225g (8oz / 1⅔ cups) self-raising white
  or wholemeal flour
½ tsp ground nutmeg or cinnamon
2 large bananas
a squeeze of lemon juice

1   Remove the kneading blade from the bread pan. Remove the bread pan from the machine, grease and line the base and sides of the pan and set aside.

2   Place the butter, sugar and honey in a bowl and beat together until light and fluffy. Gradually beat in the eggs, then fold in the flour and nutmeg or cinnamon. Peel the bananas and mash the flesh with a little lemon juice. Fold the mashed bananas into the loaf mixture until well mixed, then spoon the mixture into the bread pan and level the surface.

3   Place the bread pan in position in the machine and close the lid. Set the machine to "Bake Only" for 60 minutes. Press Start.

4   After baking, a fine skewer inserted in the centre of the loaf should come out clean. If the loaf requires further baking, bake on the same setting for a further 5–10 minutes, or until cooked.

5   Remove the bread pan from the machine using oven gloves, then leave to stand for 5 minutes, before turning the loaf out onto a wire rack to cool. Serve warm or cold in slices.

malted fruit loaf

PREPARATION TIME 20 MINUTES   **COOKING TIME** 40–50 MINUTES   **MAKES** 1 LOAF (SERVES 10–12)

225g (8oz / 1⅔ cups) self-raising white flour
1 tsp bicarbonate of soda
1 tsp ground mixed spice
3 tbsp malt extract
2 tbsp golden syrup

125ml (4fl oz / ½ cup) milk
1 egg, beaten
140g (5oz / ¾ cup) sultanas
2 tbsp clear honey, for glazing

1   Remove the kneading blade from the bread pan. Remove the bread pan from the machine, grease and line the base and sides of the pan and set aside.

2   Sift the flour, bicarbonate of soda and mixed spice into a bowl and set aside. Place the malt extract, syrup and milk in a saucepan and heat gently until melted and blended, stirring occasionally. Remove from the heat and cool slightly, then mix in the egg.

3   Make a well in the centre of the dry ingredients, then add the melted mixture, mixing well with a wooden spoon. Fold in the sultanas. Spoon the mixture into the bread pan and level the surface.

4   Place the bread pan in position in the machine and close the lid. Set the machine to "Bake Only" for 40 minutes. Press Start.

5   After baking, a fine skewer inserted in the centre of the loaf should come out clean. If the loaf requires further baking, bake on the same setting for a further 5–10 minutes, or until cooked.

6   Remove the bread pan from the machine using oven gloves, then leave to stand for 5 minutes, before turning the loaf out onto a wire rack to cool. While the loaf is still warm, brush it twice with honey to glaze. Serve warm or cold in slices.

celery & walnut loaf

PREPARATION TIME 25 MINUTES   **COOKING TIME** 45–55 MINUTES   **MAKES** 1 LOAF (SERVES 8–10)

225g (8oz / 1⅔ cups) self-raising white flour
1 tsp baking powder
55g (2oz) butter, diced
2 sticks celery, finely chopped
55g (2oz / ½ cup) walnuts, finely chopped

85g (3oz / ⅔ cup) mature Cheddar cheese,
   finely grated
sea salt and freshly ground black pepper
1 egg, beaten
about 4 tbsp milk

1   Remove the kneading blade from the bread pan. Remove the bread pan from the machine, grease and line the base and sides of the pan and set aside.

2   Sift the flour and baking powder into a bowl, then lightly rub in the butter until the mixture resembles breadcrumbs. Stir in the celery, walnuts, cheese and seasoning and mix well. Mix in the egg and enough milk to form a soft, but not sticky, dough. Turn the dough onto a lightly floured surface and knead gently until smooth. Shape to fit the bread pan and place it in the pan.

3   Place the bread pan in position in the machine and close the lid. Set the machine to "Bake Only" for 45 minutes. Press Start.

4   After baking, a fine skewer inserted in the centre of the loaf should come out clean. If the loaf requires further baking, bake on the same setting for a further 5–10 minutes, or until cooked.

5   Remove the bread pan from the machine using oven gloves, then leave to stand for 5 minutes, before turning the loaf out onto a wire rack to cool. Serve warm or cold in slices, spread with butter.

fruit & spice bread

PREPARATION TIME 20 MINUTES   **COOKING TIME** 1 HOUR–1 HOUR 10 MINUTES   **MAKES** 1 LOAF (SERVES 10–12)

225g (8oz / 1⅓ cups) self-raising white flour
½ tsp bicarbonate of soda
1 tbsp ground mixed spice
115g (4oz / ⅔ cup packed) soft light brown sugar
115g (4oz / ⅔ cup) sultanas
115g (4oz / ⅔ cup) raisins

115g (4oz / ⅔ cup) currants
115g (4oz / ⅔ cup) ready-to-eat dried apricots,
    finely chopped
2 eggs
150ml (¼ pint / ⅔ cup) milk

1   Remove the kneading blade from the bread pan. Remove the bread pan from the machine, grease and line the base and sides of the pan and set aside.

2   Sift the flour, bicarbonate of soda and mixed spice into a bowl. Add the sugar and dried fruit and mix well. Beat the eggs and milk together and add to the fruit mixture. Beat until thoroughly mixed. Spoon the mixture into the pan and level the surface.

3   Place the bread pan in position in the machine and close the lid. Set the machine to "Bake Only" for 60 minutes. Press Start.

4   After baking, a fine skewer inserted in the centre of the loaf should come out clean. If the loaf requires further baking, bake on the same setting for a further 5–10 minutes, or until cooked.

5   Remove the bread pan from the machine using oven gloves, then leave to stand for 5 minutes, before turning the loaf out onto a wire rack to cool. Serve warm or cold in slices.

CHAPTER 5

speciality & festive breads

Speciality breads are made from yeasted doughs that are enriched with a combination of other ingredients, such as eggs, sugar, butter, dried fruit or chocolate. Enriched breads, both sweet and savoury, vary in texture from soft and airy loaves with a rich and buttery flavour, to deliciously light and flaky, melt-in-the-mouth yeasted pastries, all of which are hard to resist.

Some speciality breads, such as Challah, Stollen and Panettone, are traditionally baked to celebrate a particular festival or celebration.

We include a delicious selection of enriched, speciality breads from all over the world, among them Orange & Cinnamon Brioche and Pains au Chocolat, as well as tempting delights such as Croissants, Doughnuts and Coconut Bread. We also include some simpler enriched dough recipes such as Devonshire Splits, Bath Buns and Chelsea Buns.

paradise plait

PREPARATION TIME 20 MINUTES, PLUS MIXING & KNEADING TIME IN BREADMACHINE, PLUS RISING

COOKING TIME 45–50 MINUTES   **MAKES** 1 LOAF (SERVES 10)

165ml (5½fl oz / ⅔ cup) milk (at room temperature)
2 large eggs, lightly beaten
450g (1lb / 3 cups) strong plain white flour
½ tsp salt
55g (2oz / ¼ cup) caster sugar
55g (2oz) butter, diced, plus 25g (1oz) melted
1 sachet (7g / ¼oz) fast-action dried yeast

55g (2oz / ⅓ cup) dried pineapple, chopped
115g (4oz / ⅔ cup) ready-to-eat dried pears,
    chopped
55g (2oz) blanched almonds, chopped
sifted icing sugar, for dusting

1   Whisk the milk and eggs in a bowl and pour into the bread pan. Sprinkle over the flour, covering the
    liquid completely. Place the salt, caster sugar and diced butter in separate corners of the pan. Make
    a small indent in the centre of the flour and add the yeast. Close the lid, set the machine to "Basic
    Raisin Dough" (or equivalent), or "Dough", and press Start.

2   Add the pineapple, pears and almonds when the machine makes a sound (beeps) to add extra
    ingredients during the kneading cycle (or add 5 minutes before the end of the kneading cycle).
    Meanwhile, grease a baking sheet and set aside.

3   When the dough is ready, remove it from the machine, knock it back on a lightly floured surface, then
    divide the dough into 3 equal pieces. Roll each piece of dough into a long sausage or rope shape,
    about 30cm (12in) long. Plait the dough ropes together, pressing them together at both ends to seal.
    Place on the baking sheet. Cover and leave to rise in a warm place until almost doubled in size.

4   Preheat the oven to 190°C/375°F/gas mark 5. Bake the plait for about 45–50 minutes, or until risen
    and golden brown, covering it loosely with foil towards the end of the cooking time if the top is
    browning too quickly.

5   Transfer to a wire rack to cool slightly, then brush with the melted butter and dust with icing sugar.
    Serve warm or cold in slices.

devonshire splits

PREPARATION TIME 15 MINUTES, PLUS MIXING & KNEADING TIME IN BREADMACHINE, PLUS RISING
COOKING TIME 15 MINUTES **MAKES** 10 DEVONSHIRE SPLITS

210ml (7½fl oz / ¾ cup) milk
   (at room temperature)
350g (12oz / 2½ cups) strong plain white flour
½ tsp salt
40g (1½oz / scant ¼ cup) caster sugar

40g (1½oz) butter, diced
1½ tsp fast-action dried yeast
strawberry or raspberry jam and clotted cream,
   to serve
sifted icing sugar, for dusting

1 Pour the milk into the bread pan. Sprinkle over the flour, covering the milk completely. Place the salt, caster sugar and butter in separate corners of the pan. Make a small indent in the centre of the flour and add the yeast. Close the lid, set the machine to "Dough" and press Start.

2 Meanwhile, grease 2 baking sheets and set aside. When the dough is ready, remove it from the machine, knock it back on a lightly floured surface, then divide the dough into 10 equal portions and roll each portion into a ball. Place the dough balls on the baking sheets and flatten them slightly. Cover and leave to rise in a warm place until doubled in size.

3 Preheat the oven to 220°C/425°F/gas mark 7. Bake the buns for about 15 minutes, or until they feel soft and sound hollow when tapped underneath. Transfer to a wire rack to cool.

4 Split each bun at an angle and fill with jam and cream. Dust with icing sugar just before serving.

pesto parmesan pull-apart

PREPARATION TIME 20 MINUTES, PLUS MIXING & KNEADING TIME IN BREADMACHINE, PLUS RISING
COOKING TIME 30–35 MINUTES   **MAKES** 1 LOAF (SERVES 16)

315ml (10½ fl oz / 1¼ cups) water
450g (1lb / 3 cups) strong plain white flour
1¼ tsp salt
1½ tsp caster sugar

1½ tsp fast-action dried yeast
3 tbsp ready-made green pesto sauce
40g (1½oz / ¼ cup) fresh Parmesan cheese, finely grated
beaten egg, for glazing

1   Pour the water into the bread pan. Sprinkle over the flour, covering the water completely. Place the salt and sugar in separate corners of the pan. Make a small indent in the centre of the flour and add the yeast. Close the lid, set the machine to "Dough" and press Start.

2   Meanwhile, grease a deep 23cm (9in) round cake tin and set aside. When the dough is ready, remove it from the machine, knock it back on a lightly floured surface, then roll out the dough to form a 40 x 28cm (16 x 11in) rectangle.

3   Spread the pesto sauce evenly over the dough, then sprinkle with the Parmesan cheese. Starting from a long side, roll up the dough fairly tightly like a Swiss roll. Cut into 16 even slices, then place the rolls, cut-side up, in a circular pattern in the cake tin. Cover and leave to rise in a warm place until doubled in size.

4   Preheat the oven to 200°C/400°F/gas mark 6. Brush the spirals with beaten egg, then bake for 30–35 minutes, or until deep golden brown. Cool slightly in the tin, then turn out onto a wire rack to cool completely. Pull the rolls apart to serve and serve warm or cold.

cheese & herb tear 'n' share

PREPARATION TIME 15 MINUTES, PLUS MIXING & KNEADING TIME IN BREADMACHINE, PLUS RISING

COOKING TIME 40 MINUTES   **MAKES** 1 LOAF (SERVES 12)

325ml (11fl oz / 1⅓ cups) warm water (or according
   to bread-mix packet instructions)
500g (1lb 2oz) packet white bread mix
100g (3½ oz) butter, melted
1 large egg, lightly beaten

25g (1oz) fresh Parmesan cheese, grated
2 cloves garlic, crushed
½ tsp salt
¼ tsp freshly ground black pepper
2 tsp dried herbes de Provence

1   Pour the correct amount of water into the bread pan. Sprinkle over the bread mix, covering the water
    completely. Close the lid, set the machine to "Dough" and press Start.

2   Meanwhile, grease a deep 20cm (8in) round cake tin and set aside. When the dough is ready, remove
    it from the machine, knock it back on a lightly floured surface, then divide the dough into 12 equal
    portions and roll each portion into a ball.

3   Combine the melted butter, egg, Parmesan cheese, garlic, salt, black pepper and dried herbs in a
    small bowl. Dip the dough balls into the butter mixture, coating them liberally all over, then arrange
    them in a single layer in the cake tin. Drizzle over any remaining butter mixture. Cover and leave to
    rise in a warm place for about 45 minutes, or until doubled in size.

4   Preheat the oven to 190°C/375°F/gas mark 5. Bake the loaf for about 40 minutes, or until golden
    brown. Turn out and cool on a wire rack. Pull the rolls apart to serve and serve warm or cold.

coconut bread

PREPARATION TIME 10 MINUTES   **COOKING TIME** VARIES ACCORDING TO BREADMACHINE
MAKES 1 LOAF (SERVES 10–12)

330ml (11fl oz / 1⅓ cups) milk (at room temperature)
1 tsp vanilla extract
450g (1lb / 3 cups) strong plain white flour
55g (2oz / ½ cup) desiccated coconut

1½ tsp salt
1 tbsp caster sugar
15g (½oz) butter, diced
1½ tsp fast-action dried yeast

1   Pour the milk into the bread pan and add the vanilla extract. Sprinkle over the flour, covering the milk completely, then sprinkle over the coconut. Place the salt, sugar and butter in separate corners of the pan. Make a small indent in the centre of the flour and add the yeast.

2   Close the lid, set the machine to "Sweet" or "Basic White"/"Normal" (or equivalent), then select the loaf size and crust type. Press Start.

3   After baking, remove the bread pan from the machine and turn the loaf out onto a wire rack to cool. Serve in slices.

monkey bread

PREPARATION TIME 25 MINUTES, PLUS OVERNIGHT SOAKING, PLUS MIXING & KNEADING TIME IN BREADMACHINE, PLUS RISING **COOKING TIME** 40 MINUTES **MAKES** 1 LOAF (SERVES 16)

115g (4oz / ⅔ cup) sultanas
4 tbsp brandy
175ml (6fl oz / ⅔ cup) milk (at room temperature)
3½ tbsp water
1 large egg, lightly beaten
450g (1lb / 3 cups) strong plain white flour
½ tsp salt

2 tsp caster sugar
1 sachet (7g / ¼ oz) fast-action dried yeast
115g (4oz / scant 1 cup) walnuts, finely chopped
1½ tsp ground mixed spice
115g (4oz / ⅔ cup packed) soft light brown sugar
85g (3oz) butter, melted

1 Place the sultanas in a bowl, add the brandy and stir. Leave to soak overnight.

2 Pour the milk and water into a bowl, add the egg and whisk well. Pour the mixture into the bread pan. Sprinkle over the flour, covering the liquid completely. Place the salt and caster sugar in separate corners of the pan. Make a small indent in the centre of the flour and add the yeast. Close the lid, set the machine to "Dough" and press Start.

3 Meanwhile, grease a 23cm (9in) loose-bottomed springform tin fitted with a tube base, or a ring mould, and set aside. Mix the walnuts, mixed spice and brown sugar in a bowl and set aside. When the dough is ready, remove it from the machine, knock it back on a lightly floured surface, then divide the dough into 32 pieces and roll each piece into a ball.

4 Dip each ball of dough into the melted butter, then roll in the walnut mixture, covering completely. Place half the balls in the tin, spacing them slightly apart. Spoon over the soaked sultanas and any remaining walnut mixture. Top with the rest of the dough balls and drizzle over any remaining butter. Cover and leave to rise in a warm place for about 45 minutes, or until doubled in size.

5 Preheat the oven to 190°C/375°F/gas mark 5. Bake the loaf for about 40 minutes, or until risen and golden brown. Cool in the tin for 10 minutes, then invert onto a serving plate. Pull the rolls apart to serve and serve warm or cold.

challah

PREPARATION TIME 20 MINUTES, PLUS MIXING & KNEADING TIME IN BREADMACHINE, PLUS RISING
COOKING TIME 35–40 MINUTES **MAKES** 1 LOAF (SERVES 10)

155ml (5fl oz / ⅔ cup) water
5 tbsp olive oil
2 eggs, lightly beaten
500g (1lb 2oz / 3½ cups) strong plain white flour
1½ tsp salt

1 tbsp caster sugar
1 sachet (/g / ¼oz) fast-action dried yeast
beaten egg, for glazing
sesame or poppy seeds, for sprinkling

1 Pour the water into a bowl, add the oil and eggs and whisk well. Pour the mixture into the bread pan. Sprinkle over the flour, covering the liquid completely. Place the salt and sugar in separate corners of the pan. Make a small indent in the centre of the flour and add the yeast. Close the lid, set the machine to "Dough" and press Start.

2 Meanwhile, grease a large baking sheet and set aside. When the dough is ready, remove it from the machine, knock it back on a lightly floured surface, then divide the dough into 4 equal portions.

3 Roll each portion of the dough into a rope about 40cm (16in) long. Place the ropes of dough side by side and pinch them together at one end. Starting from the right, make a plait, lifting the first rope over the second and the third rope over the fourth, then placing the fourth rope between the first and second ropes. Repeat and continue, to form a plait, pinching the ends together when you have finished. Tuck the ends under at each end of the plait and place the plait on the baking sheet. Cover and leave to rise in a warm place until doubled in size.

4 Preheat the oven to 220°C/425°F/gas mark 7. Brush the dough with beaten egg and sprinkle with sesame or poppy seeds. Bake for 15 minutes, then reduce the oven temperature to 190°C/375°F/gas mark 5 and bake for a further 20–25 minutes, or until risen and golden brown. Transfer to a wire rack to cool. Serve in slices or wedges.

orange & cinnamon brioche

PREPARATION TIME 25 MINUTES, PLUS MIXING & KNEADING TIME IN BREADMACHINE, PLUS RISING
COOKING TIME 30 MINUTES   **MAKES** 1 LOAF (SERVES 12–14)

150g (5½oz) butter
3 large eggs, lightly beaten
2 tbsp milk
1 tbsp finely grated orange zest
450g (1lb / 3 cups) strong plain white flour

1 tsp ground cinnamon
1 tsp salt
55g (2oz / ¼ cup) caster sugar
1 sachet (7g / ¼oz) fast-action dried yeast
beaten egg yolk, for glazing

1   Melt 75g (2¾oz) of the butter. Whisk the melted butter, eggs, milk and orange zest together in a bowl, then pour into the bread pan. Sprinkle over the flour, covering the liquid completely, then sprinkle over the cinnamon. Place the salt, sugar and remaining butter in separate corners of the pan. Make a small indent in the centre of the flour and add the yeast. Close the lid, set the machine to "Dough" and press Start.

2   Grease a 1.7 litre (3 pint) brioche tin and set aside. When the dough is ready, remove it from the machine, knock it back on a lightly floured surface, then cut a quarter from the dough and set aside. Knead the remaining piece of dough, shape it into a large ball and place it in the tin.

3   Shape the reserved piece of dough into a pear shape. Make a hollow in the centre of the large round of dough and place the thinner end of the pear-shaped piece of dough into the hollow. Cover and leave to rise in a warm place until the dough nearly reaches the top of the tin.

4   Preheat the oven to 200°C/400°F/gas mark 6. Brush the brioche with beaten egg yolk, then bake for about 30 minutes, or until risen and golden. Turn out and cool on a wire rack. Serve warm or cold.

bath buns

PREPARATION TIME 15 MINUTES, PLUS MIXING & KNEADING TIME IN BREADMACHINE, PLUS RISING
COOKING TIME 20 MINUTES   **MAKES** ABOUT 16 BUNS

150ml (¼ pint / ⅔ cup) milk (at room temperature)
2 eggs, lightly beaten
55g (2oz) butter, melted
500g (1lb 2oz / 3½ cups) strong plain white flour
1 tsp salt
55g (2oz / ¼ cup) caster sugar

2 tsp fast-action dried yeast
175g (6oz / 1 cup) sultanas
55g (2oz / ⅓ cup) chopped mixed peel
beaten egg, for glazing
25g (1oz) sugar cubes, coarsely crushed

1   Whisk the milk, eggs and melted butter in a bowl, then pour into the bread pan. Sprinkle over the flour, covering the liquid completely. Place the salt and caster sugar in separate corners of the pan. Make a small indent in the centre of the flour and add the yeast. Close the lid, set the machine to "Basic Raisin Dough" (or equivalent), or "Dough", and press Start.

2   Add the sultanas and mixed peel when the machine makes a sound (beeps) to add extra ingredients during the kneading cycle (or add 5 minutes before the end of the kneading cycle). Meanwhile, grease 2 baking sheets and set aside.

3   When the dough is ready, remove it from the machine, knock it back on a lightly floured surface, then divide the dough into about 16 equal portions. Knead each portion of the dough into a ball and place on the baking sheets. Flatten each ball slightly. Cover and leave to rise in a warm place until doubled in size.

4   Preheat the oven to 190°C/375°F/gas mark 5. Brush the tops of the buns with beaten egg and sprinkle with the crushed sugar cubes. Bake for about 20 minutes, or until risen and golden brown. Transfer to a wire rack to cool and serve warm or cold on their own or split and spread with butter.

lardy cake

PREPARATION TIME 25 MINUTES, PLUS MIXING & KNEADING TIME IN BREADMACHINE, PLUS RISING
COOKING TIME 30 MINUTES   **MAKES** 1 CAKE (SERVES 10–12)

300ml (½ pint / 1¼ cups) water
450g (1lb / 3 cups) strong plain white flour
1 tsp salt
25g (1oz / 2 tbsp) caster sugar, plus 1 tbsp
    for the glaze
150g (5½oz) lard
1½ tsp fast-action dried yeast

115g (4oz / ⅔ cup packed) soft light brown sugar
85g (3oz / ½ cup) currants
85g (3oz / ½ cup) sultanas
55g (2oz / ⅓ cup) chopped mixed peel
1 tsp ground mixed spice
1 tbsp boiling water

1 Pour the water into the bread pan. Sprinkle over the flour, covering the water completely. Place
   the salt, caster sugar and 15g (½oz) of the lard in separate corners of the pan. Make a small indent in
   the centre of the flour and add the yeast. Close the lid, set the machine to "Dough" and press Start.
   Meanwhile, grease a 25 x 20cm (10 x 8in) shallow roasting tin and set aside.

2 When the dough is ready, remove it from the machine, knock it back on a floured surface, then roll out
   the dough to form a rectangle about 5mm (¼in) thick. With a short side of the rectangle nearest to
   you, dot the top two-thirds of the dough with flakes of one-third of the remaining lard. Sprinkle over
   one-third each of the brown sugar, dried fruits, mixed peel and mixed spice. Fold the bottom third of
   the dough up over the middle third, then fold the top third down over the middle third to form a parcel.
   Seal the edges with a rolling pin. Give the dough a quarter turn so the folded side is to the left.

3 Repeat this whole procedure, rolling, filling and folding the dough, twice more, using the remaining
   lard, brown sugar, dried fruits, mixed peel and mixed spice. Fold, seal and turn as before. Roll out the
   dough to fit the tin and place it inside. Cover and leave to rise in a warm place for about 1–1½ hours,
   or until almost doubled in size.

4 Preheat the oven to 200°C/400°F/gas mark 6. Score the top of the dough in a criss-cross pattern, then
   bake for about 30 minutes, or until risen and golden brown.

5 Dissolve the remaining 1 tbsp caster sugar in the boiling water, then brush this glaze over the top of
   the warm cake. Leave to cool in the tin for a few minutes, then turn out and serve warm or cold, cut
   into slices or squares.

panettone

PREPARATION TIME 25 MINUTES, PLUS MIXING & KNEADING TIME IN BREADMACHINE, PLUS RISING
COOKING TIME 45–50 MINUTES   **MAKES** 1 LOAF (SERVES 8–10)

3 large eggs, lightly beaten
3 tbsp milk
375g (13oz / 2⅔ cups) strong plain white flour
½ tsp salt
55g (2oz / ¼ cup) caster sugar
115g (4oz) butter, softened

2 tsp fast-action dried yeast
115g (4oz / ⅔ cup) sultanas
55g (2oz / ⅓ cup) chopped mixed peel
finely grated zest of 1 small lemon
15g (½oz) butter, melted, for glazing

1 Whisk the eggs and milk in a bowl. Pour the mixture into the bread pan. Sprinkle over the flour,
  covering the liquid completely. Place the salt and sugar in separate corners of the pan. Dot the
  softened butter over the surface, then make a small indent in the centre of the flour and add
  the yeast. Close the lid, set the machine to "Basic Raisin Dough" (or equivalent), or "Dough",
  and press Start.

2 Add the sultanas, mixed peel and lemon zest when the machine makes a sound (beeps) to add extra
  ingredients during the kneading cycle (or add 5 minutes before the end of the kneading cycle).

3 Grease and line a deep 18cm (7in) round cake tin. Tie a double layer of greaseproof paper around the
  outside of the tin, with string, making the collar about 7.5cm (3in) above the rim. Set aside.

4 When the dough is ready, remove it from the machine, knock it back on a lightly floured surface, then
  shape the dough into a round. Place in the tin and cut a cross in the top. Cover and leave to rise in a
  warm place until doubled in size.

5 Preheat the oven to 200°C/400°F/gas mark 6. Brush the top of the dough with the melted butter. Bake
  for 15 minutes, then reduce the oven temperature to 180°C/350°F/gas mark 4 and bake for a further
  30–35 minutes, or until the top is golden brown and crisp. Turn out and cool on a wire rack.

hot cross buns

PREPARATION TIME 20 MINUTES, PLUS MIXING & KNEADING TIME IN BREADMACHINE, PLUS RISING
COOKING TIME 15–20 MINUTES   **MAKES** 12–14 BUNS

250ml (9fl oz / 1 cup) milk (at room temperature)
1 large egg, lightly beaten
450g (1lb / 3 cups) strong plain white flour
1 tsp ground mixed spice
1 tsp ground cinnamon
1 tsp grated nutmeg
1 tsp salt
2 tbsp caster sugar

55g (2oz) butter, diced
1½ tsp fast-action dried yeast
finely grated zest of 1 lemon
85g (3oz / ½ cup) sultanas
25g (1oz) chopped mixed peel
85g (3oz) ready-made shortcrust pastry
55g (2oz / ¼ cup) granulated sugar
3 tbsp water

1   Pour the milk into a bowl, add the egg and whisk well. Pour the mixture into the bread pan. Sprinkle over the flour, covering the liquid completely, then sprinkle over the ground spices. Place the salt, caster sugar and butter in separate corners of the pan. Make a small indent in the centre of the flour and add the yeast. Close the lid, set the machine to "Basic Raisin Dough" (or equivalent), or "Dough", and press Start.

2   Add the lemon zest, sultanas and mixed peel when the machine makes a sound (beeps) to add extra ingredients during the kneading cycle (or add 5 minutes before the end of the kneading cycle). Meanwhile, grease 2 baking sheets and set aside.

3   When the dough is ready, remove it from the machine, knock it back on a lightly floured surface, then divide the dough into 12 or 14 equal portions.

4   Knead each portion into a ball and place on the baking sheets. Flatten each ball slightly. Roll out the pastry on a lightly floured surface and cut into narrow strips. Brush the buns with a little water and top each one with a pastry cross. Cover and leave to rise in a warm place until doubled in size.

5   Preheat the oven to 190°C/375°F/gas mark 5. Bake the buns for about 15–20 minutes, or until golden. Transfer to a wire rack.

6   Meanwhile, make the glaze. Dissolve the granulated sugar in a saucepan with the water. Heat gently, stirring until the sugar has dissolved, then bring to the boil and boil rapidly for 2 minutes. As soon as the buns come out of the oven, brush them twice with the sugar glaze. Leave to cool and serve warm or cold.

croissants

PREPARATION TIME 35 MINUTES, PLUS MIXING & KNEADING TIME IN BREADMACHINE, PLUS RISING
COOKING TIME 15–20 MINUTES **MAKES** 12 CROISSANTS

300ml (½ pint / 1¼ cups) milk (at room temperature)
500g (1lb 2oz / 3½ cups) strong plain white flour
1 tsp salt
2 tbsp caster sugar

280g (10oz) butter (at room temperature)
1 sachet (7g / ¼oz) fast-action dried yeast
beaten egg, for glazing

1. Pour the milk into the bread pan. Sprinkle over the flour, covering the milk completely. Place the salt, sugar and 55g (2oz) of the butter in separate corners of the pan. Make a small indent in the centre of the flour and add the yeast. Close the lid, set the machine to "Dough" and press Start.

2. Meanwhile, grease 2 baking sheets and set aside. When the dough is ready, remove it from the machine, knock it back on a lightly floured surface, then roll out the dough to form a rectangle about 35 x 18cm (14 x 7in).

3. Flatten the remaining butter into a block about 2cm (¾in) thick. With a short side of the dough rectangle nearest to you, place the butter on top of the dough so that it covers the top two-thirds of the rectangle. Fold the bottom third of the dough over the middle third, then fold the top buttered third down over the top of the middle third to form a parcel. Seal the edges with a rolling pin.

4. Give the dough a quarter turn so the folded side is to the left. Roll into a rectangle as before, then fold the bottom third up and the top third down and seal the edges, as before. Wrap in greaseproof paper and chill in the refrigerator for 20 minutes. Repeat the rolling, folding and chilling twice more, turning the dough 90 degrees each time before rolling.

5. Roll out the dough on a lightly floured surface to form a 53 x 35cm (21 x 14in) rectangle and cut into 12 equal triangles. Roll each triangle into a sausage shape, starting from the long side and ending with the point of the triangle. Bend the ends of each croissant round to make a crescent or half-moon shape. Place on the baking sheets. Cover and leave to rise in a warm place for about 30 minutes, or until almost doubled in size.

6. Preheat the oven to 220°C/425°F/gas mark 7. Lightly brush the croissants with beaten egg, then bake for 15–20 minutes, or until crisp and golden brown. Serve warm.

chelsea buns

PREPARATION TIME 20 MINUTES, PLUS MIXING & KNEADING TIME IN BREADMACHINE, PLUS RISING

COOKING TIME 25–30 MINUTES   **MAKES** 12 BUNS

100ml (3½fl oz / ⅓ cup) milk (at room temperature)
1 large egg, lightly beaten
225g (8oz / 1½ cups) strong plain white flour
½ tsp salt
2 tbsp caster sugar
55g (2oz) butter, diced

1 tsp fast-action dried yeast
85g (3oz / ½ cup) mixed raisins and currants
55g (2oz / ⅓ cup) sultanas
55g (2oz / ¼ cup packed) soft light brown sugar
1½ tsp ground cinnamon
2 tbsp clear honey, for glazing

1   Whisk the milk and egg together in a bowl and pour into the bread pan. Sprinkle over the flour, covering the liquid completely. Place the salt, caster sugar and 25g (1oz) of the butter in separate corners of the pan. Make a small indent in the centre of the flour and add the yeast. Close the lid, set the machine to "Dough" and press Start.

2   Grease an 18cm (7in) square cake tin and set aside. When the dough is ready, remove it from the machine, knock it back on a lightly floured surface, then roll it out into a 30 x 23cm (12 x 9in) rectangle.

3   Melt the remaining butter and brush it over the dough. Combine the dried fruit, brown sugar and cinnamon and sprinkle evenly over the dough, leaving a 2.5cm (1in) border around the edges.

4   Starting from a long side, roll up the dough fairly tightly like a Swiss roll. Cut into 12 even slices and place, cut-sides up, in the tin. Cover and leave to rise in a warm place until doubled in size.

5   Preheat the oven to 190°C/375°F/gas mark 5. Bake the buns for about 25–30 minutes, or until risen and golden brown. Remove from the oven and brush twice with honey while still hot. Cool slightly, then turn out onto a wire rack. Serve warm or cold.

easter bread ring

PREPARATION TIME 25 MINUTES, PLUS MIXING & KNEADING TIME IN BREADMACHINE, PLUS RISING

COOKING TIME 20–25 MINUTES   **MAKES** 1 RING (SERVES 10–12)

100ml (3½fl oz / ⅓ cup) milk (at room temperature), plus extra for glazing
1 large egg, lightly beaten
225g (8oz / 1½ cups) strong plain white flour
½ tsp salt
2 tbsp caster sugar
55g (2oz) butter, diced
1 tsp fast-action dried yeast

85g (3oz / ½ cup) sultanas
85g (3oz / ½ cup) ready-to-eat dried apricots, chopped
55g (2oz / ¼ cup packed) soft light brown sugar
1½ tsp ground mixed spice
115g (4oz / scant 1 cup) icing sugar, sifted
about 4 tsp water
25g (1oz / ¼ cup) toasted flaked almonds

1   Whisk the milk and egg in a bowl and pour into the pan. Sprinkle over the flour, covering the liquid completely. Place the salt, caster sugar and 25g (1oz) of the butter in separate corners of the pan. Make a small indent in the centre of the flour and add the yeast. Close the lid, set the machine to "Dough" and press Start.

2   Grease a baking sheet and set aside. When the dough is ready, remove it from the machine, knock it back on a lightly floured surface, then roll it out into a 46 x 30cm (18 x 12in) rectangle. Melt the remaining butter and brush it over the dough. Sprinkle with the fruit, brown sugar and spice.

3   Starting from a long side, roll up the dough like a Swiss roll, then shape it into a circle, seam-side down. Brush the ends with milk and press them together to seal. Place the dough ring on the baking sheet.

4   Using a sharp knife, make cuts two-thirds of the way through the dough at 4cm (1½in) intervals, twisting the slices outwards at an angle so they overlap slightly. Cover and leave to rise in a warm place until doubled in size.

5   Preheat the oven to 200°C/400°F/gas mark 6. Bake for 20–25 minutes, or until golden brown. Transfer to a wire rack to cool. Mix the icing sugar with the water to make a thin glacé icing and drizzle it over the warm baked ring. Sprinkle with the almonds. Serve warm or cold in slices.

doughnuts

PREPARATION TIME 20 MINUTES, PLUS MIXING & KNEADING TIME IN BREADMACHINE, PLUS RISING
COOKING TIME 25 MINUTES   **MAKES** 16 DOUGHNUTS

175ml (6fl oz / ⅔ cup) milk (at room temperature)
2 large eggs, lightly beaten
500g (1lb 2oz / 3½ cups) strong plain white flour
1 tsp salt
175g (6oz / ¾ cup) caster sugar

25g (1oz) butter, diced
1½ tsp fast-action dried yeast
115g (4oz / ⅓ cup) strawberry or raspberry jam
sunflower oil, for deep frying
1½ tsp ground cinnamon

1   Pour the milk into a bowl, add the eggs and whisk well. Pour the mixture into the bread pan. Sprinkle over the flour, covering the liquid completely. Place the salt, 85g (3oz) of the sugar and the butter in separate corners of the pan. Make a small indent in the centre of the flour and add the yeast. Close the lid, set the machine to "Dough" and press Start.

2   Meanwhile, oil 2 baking sheets and set aside. When the dough is ready, remove it from the machine, knock it back on a lightly floured surface, then divide the dough into 16 equal portions.

3   Shape each portion of the dough into a ball, then flatten each one into a disc about 1cm (½in) thick. Place 1 heaped teaspoon of jam into the middle of each disc, gather the edges of the dough up and over the jam, enclosing it completely, then pinch the edges firmly together to seal, and roll into a ball. Place on the baking sheets, cover and leave to rise in a warm place for about 30 minutes, or until almost doubled in size.

4   Heat some oil in a deep-fat fryer to 170°C/325°F and fry the doughnuts in batches in the hot oil for about 6 minutes, or until golden all over, turning once. Remove the doughnuts from the fryer using a slotted spoon and drain on kitchen paper.

5   Combine the remaining sugar and the cinnamon in a bowl and toss the doughnuts in the sugar mixture, coating them all over. Serve immediately.

pains au chocolat

PREPARATION TIME 35 MINUTES, PLUS MIXING & KNEADING TIME IN BREADMACHINE, PLUS RISING
COOKING TIME 15–20 MINUTES   **MAKES** 12 PAINS AU CHOCOLAT

300ml (½ pint / 1¼ cups) milk (at room temperature)
500g (1lb 2oz / 3½ cups) strong plain white flour
1 tsp salt
2 tbsp caster sugar

280g (10oz) butter (at room temperature)
1 sachet (7g / ¼oz) fast-action dried yeast
175g (6oz) plain or milk chocolate, finely chopped
beaten egg, for glazing

1   Pour the milk into the bread pan. Sprinkle over the flour, covering the milk completely. Place the salt, sugar and 55g (2oz) of the butter in separate corners of the pan. Make a small indent in the centre of the flour and add the yeast. Close the lid, set the machine to "Dough" and press Start.

2   Grease 2 baking sheets and set aside. When the dough is ready, remove it from the machine, knock it back on a lightly floured surface, then roll out the dough to form a rectangle about 53 x 35cm (21 x 14in).

3   Flatten the remaining butter into a block about 2cm (¾in) thick. With a short side of the dough rectangle nearest to you, place the butter on top of the dough so that it covers the top two-thirds of the rectangle. Fold the bottom third of the dough over the middle third, then fold the top buttered third down over the top of the middle third to form a parcel. Seal the edges with a rolling pin.

4   Give the dough a quarter turn so the folded side is to the left. Roll into a rectangle as before, then fold the bottom third up and the top third down and seal the edges, as before. Wrap in greaseproof paper and chill in the refrigerator for 20 minutes. Repeat the rolling, folding and chilling twice more, turning the dough 90 degrees each time, before rolling.

5   Roll out the dough on a lightly floured surface to form a 53 x 35cm (21 x 14in) rectangle and cut into 12 equal rectangles. Place 15g (½oz) of the chopped chocolate at one end of each rectangle. Roll up each rectangle to make a flattish cylinder shape, enclosing the chocolate completely. Place seam-side down on the baking sheets. Cover and leave to rise in a warm place until almost doubled in size.

6   Preheat the oven to 200°C/400°F/gas mark 6. Lightly brush the pastries with beaten egg, then bake for 15–20 minutes, or until crisp and golden brown. Serve warm.

danish apple plait

PREPARATION TIME 25 MINUTES, PLUS MIXING & KNEADING TIME IN BREADMACHINE, PLUS RISING
COOKING TIME 20–25 MINUTES   **MAKES** 1 LOAF (SERVES 8)

100ml (3½fl oz / ⅓ cup) milk (at room temperature)
1 large egg, lightly beaten
250g (9oz / 1¾ cups) strong plain white flour
½ tsp salt
25g (1oz) butter, diced
55g (2oz / ¼ cup) caster sugar
1 tsp fast-action dried yeast
140g (5oz) ready-made marzipan or almond paste,
   coarsely grated

1 large or 2 small cooking apples, peeled, cored
   and thinly sliced
1 tsp ground cinnamon
beaten egg, for glazing
85g (3oz / ⅔ cup) icing sugar, sifted
15g (½oz) toasted flaked almonds or chopped
   pistachio nuts, to decorate

1   Whisk the milk and egg in a bowl and pour into the bread pan. Sprinkle over the flour, covering the
    liquid completely. Place the salt, butter and 25g (1oz / 2 tbsp) of the caster sugar in separate corners
    of the pan. Make a small indent in the centre of the flour and add the yeast. Close the lid, set the
    machine to "Dough" and press Start

2   Grease a baking sheet and set aside. When the dough is ready, remove it from the machine, knock it
    back on a lightly floured surface, then roll it out to form a 30 x 25cm (12 x 10in) rectangle. Place the
    marzipan evenly down the centre third (lengthways) of the dough (about 6–7.5cm/2½–3in wide).

3   Toss the apple slices with the remaining caster sugar and the cinnamon, then spoon this mixture
    evenly over the marzipan. On the longest sides of the dough, make diagonal cuts up to the filling at
    2.5cm (1in) intervals. Plait the strips of dough over the filling, pressing lightly to seal. Tuck the ends
    under to seal at both ends of the plait. Place the plait on the baking sheet, then cover and leave to
    rise in a warm place until doubled in size.

4   Preheat the oven to 200°C/400°F/gas mark 6. Lightly brush the plait with beaten egg, then bake for
    about 20–25 minutes, or until risen and golden. Transfer to a wire rack to cool.

5   Blend the icing sugar with a little water to make a thin glacé icing. Drizzle the icing over the warm
    plait, then sprinkle with almonds or pistachio nuts. Serve warm or cold in slices.

stollen

PREPARATION TIME 25 MINUTES, PLUS MIXING & KNEADING TIME IN BREADMACHINE, PLUS RISING
COOKING TIME 40 MINUTES   **MAKES** 1 LOAF (SERVES 10–12)

150ml (¼ pint / ⅔ cup) milk (at room temperature)
1 large egg, lightly beaten
350g (12oz / 2½ cups) strong plain white flour
1 tsp ground mixed spice
½ tsp salt
2 tbsp caster sugar
40g (1½oz) butter, diced

1½ tsp fast-action dried yeast
175g (6oz / 1 cup) luxury mixed dried fruit
55g (2oz / ½ cup) blanched almonds, finely chopped
finely grated zest of 1 lemon
175g (6oz) ready-made marzipan or almond paste
icing sugar and ground cinnamon, for dusting

1   Whisk the milk and egg in a bowl and pour into the bread pan. Sprinkle over the flour, covering
    the liquid completely, then sprinkle over the mixed spice. Place the salt, caster sugar and butter in
    separate corners of the pan. Make a small indent in the centre of the flour and add the yeast. Close
    the lid, set the machine to "Basic Raisin Dough" (or equivalent), or "Dough", and press Start.

2   Mix together the dried fruit, almonds and lemon zest and set aside. Add the dried fruit mixture when
    the machine makes a sound (beeps) to add extra ingredients during the kneading cycle (or add 5
    minutes before the end of the kneading cycle).

3   Grease a baking sheet and set aside. When the dough is ready, remove it from the machine, knock it
    back on a lightly floured surface, then roll it out into a rectangle about 23 x 15cm (9 x 6in) in size.

4   Roll the marzipan into a long sausage shape, just a little shorter than the length of the rectangle, and
    place the marzipan log along the centre of the dough. Fold the dough over almost in half to enclose it
    and press the edges together to seal. Transfer to the baking sheet, cover and leave to rise in a warm
    place until doubled in size.

5   Preheat the oven to 180°C/350°F/gas mark 4. Bake the loaf for about 40 minutes, or until deep golden
    brown. Transfer to a wire rack to cool. Dust with a mixture of sifted icing sugar and cinnamon. Serve
    in slices.

apple & cinnamon pull-apart

PREPARATION TIME 25 MINUTES, PLUS MIXING & KNEADING TIME IN BREADMACHINE, PLUS RISING

COOKING TIME 25–30 MINUTES   **MAKES** 1 LOAF (SERVES 12)

150ml (¼ pint / ⅔ cup) milk (at room temperature)
125ml (4fl oz / ½ cup) water
1 large egg, lightly beaten
450g (1lb / 3 cups) strong plain white flour
1 tsp salt
2 tbsp caster sugar
2 tsp fast-action dried yeast

175g (6oz / scant 1 cup packed) light soft
    brown sugar
1½ tsp ground cinnamon
3 eating apples, peeled, cored and thinly sliced
4 tbsp double cream
25g (1oz) butter, diced
25g (1oz / ¼ cup) hazelnuts, finely chopped

1   Whisk the milk, water and egg in a bowl and pour into the bread pan. Sprinkle over the flour, covering the liquid completely. Place the salt and caster sugar in separate corners of the pan. Make a small indent in the centre of the flour and add the yeast. Close the lid, set the machine to "Dough" and press Start.

2   Grease a 23cm (9in) loose-bottomed springform tin fitted with a tube base, or a ring mould, and set aside. When the dough is ready, remove it from the machine, knock it back on a lightly floured surface, then roll out the dough to form a 40 x 20cm (16 x 8in) rectangle.

3   Combine 55g (2oz / ¼ cup packed) of the brown sugar and the cinnamon, then add the apple slices and toss to mix well. Spoon the mixture evenly over the dough, leaving a 1cm (½in) border around the edges. Starting from a long side, roll up the dough fairly tightly like a Swiss roll. Cut into 12 even slices, then place the slices upright but at an angle (so they rest on each other) in the tin. Cover and leave to rise in a warm place for about 1½–2 hours, or until doubled in size.

4   Preheat the oven to 190°C/375°F/gas mark 5. Bake for 25–30 minutes, or until risen and golden brown. Cool slightly in the tin, then turn out onto a wire rack.

5   Meanwhile, place the remaining brown sugar, the cream and butter in a small pan and heat gently, stirring, until the sugar has dissolved. Bring gently to the boil, then simmer, uncovered, for about 4 minutes, or until the mixture thickens slightly.

6   Brush the hot pull-apart with the caramel mixture, then sprinkle with the hazelnuts. Pull the rolls apart to serve and serve warm or cold.

CHAPTER 6

teabreads & tea-time treats

Delicious, moist teabreads are perfect for serving with a cup of tea or coffee as a tasty afternoon snack, although most can be enjoyed as a treat at any time of the day.

Teabreads are generally easy to make and those that are enriched with butter or eggs will keep well for a few days if wrapped or stored in an airtight container. Other treats, such as teacakes and muffins, should be eaten freshly baked or toasted.

Choose from iced delights such as Lemon Blueberry Loaf and Iced Orange Teabread, or enjoy munching on Marbled Chocolate Teabread and Hawaiian Fruit Teabread. For a more traditional and hard-to-resist tea-time treat, split and toast some Teacake Fingers and serve them hot, spread with melting butter.

iced raisin loaf

PREPARATION TIME 20 MINUTES, PLUS OVERNIGHT SOAKING

COOKING TIME 1¼ HOURS–1 HOUR 25 MINUTES   **MAKES** 1 LOAF (SERVES 10–12)

225g (8oz / 1¼ cups) raisins
115g (4oz / ⅔ cup) sultanas
300ml (½ pint / 1¼ cups) strong hot tea, strained
225g (8oz / 1¼ cups packed) soft light brown sugar
300g (10½oz / 2¼ cups) self-raising white flour

1½ tsp ground mixed spice
1 egg, beaten
175g (6oz / 1½ cups) icing sugar, sifted
about 5–6 tsp orange juice

1   Place the raisins and sultanas in a large bowl, pour over the hot tea and stir to mix. Cover and leave to soak overnight.

2   The next day, remove the kneading blade from the bread pan. Remove the bread pan from the machine, grease and line the base and sides of the pan and set aside. Stir the brown sugar into the fruit mixture, then sift in the flour and mixed spice. Add the egg and mix throroughly with a wooden spoon. Spoon the mixture into the bread pan and level the surface.

3   Place the bread pan in position in the machine and close the lid. Set the machine to "Bake Only" for 75 minutes. Press Start.

4   After baking, a fine skewer inserted in the centre of the loaf should come out clean. If not, bake on the same setting for a further 5–10 minutes, or until cooked.

5   Remove the bread pan from the machine using oven gloves, then leave to stand for 5 minutes, before turning the loaf out onto a wire rack to cool completely.

6   Combine the icing sugar with enough orange juice to make a thick, smooth icing. Spread the icing evenly over the top of the cold loaf. Leave to set. Serve in slices.

malted sultana loaf

PREPARATION TIME 10 MINUTES   **COOKING TIME** VARIES ACCORDING TO BREADMACHINE

MAKES 1 LOAF (SERVES 10)

350ml (12fl oz / 1⅓ cups) water
3 tbsp malt extract
500g (1lb 2oz / 3½ cups) strong plain white flour
1 tbsp skimmed milk powder
1½ tsp salt

2 tsp caster sugar
25g (1oz) butter, diced
1 tsp fast-action dried yeast
115g (4oz / ⅔ cup) sultanas

1   Pour the water into the bread pan, then add the malt extract. Sprinkle over the flour, covering the liquid completely. Sprinkle the milk powder over the flour. Place the salt, sugar and butter in separate corners of the pan. Make a small indent in the centre of the flour and add the yeast.

2   Close the lid, set the machine to "Basic White"/"Normal", with "Raisin", if available (or equivalent), then select the loaf size and crust type. Press Start.

3   Add the sultanas when the machine makes a sound (beeps) to add extra ingredients during the kneading cycle (or add 5 minutes before the end of the kneading cycle).

4   After baking, remove the bread pan from the machine, then turn the loaf out onto a wire rack to cool. Serve in slices.

Variation Use raisins, sweetened dried cranberries or chopped ready-to-eat dried apricots or pears in place of sultanas.

banana-chip muesli teabread

PREPARATION TIME 15 MINUTES   **COOKING TIME** 1–1¼ HOURS   **MAKES** 1 LOAF (SERVES 10)

175g (6oz) butter, softened
175g (6oz / scant 1 cup packed) soft light brown sugar
3 eggs, beaten
175g (6oz / 1⅓ cups) self raising white flour

55g (2oz) muesli (of your choice),
    such as Swiss-style muesli
85g (3oz / ½ cup) banana chips
sifted icing sugar, to decorate (optional)

1   Remove the kneading blade from the bread pan. Remove the bread pan from the machine, grease and line the base and sides of the pan and set aside.

2   Cream the butter and brown sugar together in a bowl until light and fluffy, then gradually beat in the eggs. Sift the flour into the bowl, then fold the flour into the creamed mixture together with the muesli and banana chips, mixing well. Spoon the mixture into the bread pan and level the surface.

3   Place the bread pan in position in the machine and close the lid. Set the machine to "Bake Only" for 60 minutes. Press Start.

4   After baking, a fine skewer inserted in the centre of the teabread should come out clean. If the loaf requires further baking, bake on the same setting for a further 10–15 minutes, or until cooked.

5   Remove the bread pan from the machine using oven gloves, then leave to stand for 10 minutes, before turning the teabread out onto a wire rack to cool. Dust with sifted icing sugar, if desired, and serve warm or cold in slices.

iced orange teabread

PREPARATION TIME 15 MINUTES **COOKING TIME** 1 HOUR–1 HOUR 10 MINUTES **MAKES** 1 LOAF (SERVES 10)

FOR THE TEABREAD
115g (4oz) butter, softened
55g (2oz / ¼ cup packed) soft light brown sugar
2 eggs, beaten
140g (5oz / 1 cup) self-raising white flour, sifted
140g (5oz / 1 cup) self-raising wholemeal flour
1½ tsp ground ginger
8 tbsp orange marmalade (about 200g / 7oz)
about 1 tbsp milk

FOR THE ICING
85g (3oz) butter, softened
1 tsp finely grated orange zest
175g (6oz / 1½ cups) icing sugar, sifted
2 tsp orange juice
thinly pared orange zest, to decorate (optional)

1 Remove the kneading blade from the bread pan. Remove the bread pan from the machine, grease and line the base and sides of the pan and set aside.

2 For the teabread, cream the butter and brown sugar together in a bowl until light and fluffy, then gradually beat in the eggs. Fold the flours and ground ginger into the creamed mixture, mixing well. Fold in the marmalade and enough milk to make a fairly soft consistency. Spoon the mixture into the bread pan and level the surface.

3 Place the bread pan in position in the machine and close the lid. Set the machine to "Bake Only" for 60 minutes. Press Start.

4 After baking, a fine skewer inserted in the centre of the teabread should come out clean. If the teabread requires further baking, bake on the same setting for a further 5–10 minutes, or until cooked.

5 Remove the bread pan from the machine using oven gloves. Leave to stand for 10 minutes, before turning the loaf out onto a wire rack to cool completely.

6 Meanwhile, make the icing. Cream the butter in a bowl until pale and fluffy, then beat in the grated orange zest. Gradually stir in the icing sugar and orange juice, mixing to make a soft icing. Spread the icing over the top of the cold loaf and sprinkle with the pared orange zest, if desired. Serve in slices.

lemon blueberry loaf

PREPARATION TIME 15 MINUTES   **COOKING TIME** 1–1¼ HOURS   **MAKES** 1 LOAF (SERVES 10)

225g (8oz / 1⅔ cups) self-raising white flour
115g (4oz) butter, diced
115g (4oz / ½ cup) caster sugar
40g (1½oz / ⅓ cup) ground almonds or hazelnuts
finely grated zest and juice of 1 lemon

2 eggs, beaten
4 tbsp milk
200g (7oz / 1½ cups) fresh blueberries,
   rinsed and dried
55g (2oz / ½ cup) icing sugar, sifted

1   Remove the kneading blade from the bread pan. Remove the bread pan from the machine, grease and line the base and sides of the pan and set aside.

2   Sift the flour into a bowl, then lightly rub in the butter. Stir in the caster sugar, nuts and lemon zest, then beat in the eggs and milk, mixing well. Fold in the blueberries. Spoon the mixture into the bread pan and level the surface.

3   Place the bread pan in position in the machine and close the lid. Set the machine to "Bake Only" for 60 minutes. Press Start.

4   After baking, a fine skewer inserted in the centre of the loaf should come out clean. If the loaf requires further baking, bake on the same setting for a further 10–15 minutes, or until cooked.

5   Remove the pan from the machine using oven gloves. Leave to stand for 10 minutes, before turning the loaf out onto a wire rack to cool completely.

6   Meanwhile, make the icing. Combine the icing sugar with 1–2 teaspoons lemon juice to make a fairly thin glacé icing. Drizzle the icing over the cold loaf. Serve in slices.

marbled chocolate teabread

PREPARATION TIME 25 MINUTES   **COOKING TIME** 55–65 MINUTES   **MAKES** 1 LOAF (SERVES 10)

175g (6oz) butter, softened
175g (6oz / scant 1 cup packed) soft light brown sugar
3 eggs, beaten
225g (8oz / 1⅔ cups) plain white flour
2½ tsp baking powder

2 ripe bananas, peeled and mashed with lemon juice
25g (1oz / ¼ cup) cocoa powder
2 tsp milk
½ tsp ground ginger
sifted icing sugar and cocoa powder, for dusting

1   Remove the kneading blade from the bread pan. Remove the bread pan from the machine, grease and line the base and sides of the pan and set aside.

2   Cream the butter and brown sugar together in a bowl. Gradually beat in the eggs. Sift over the flour and baking powder and fold in, mixing well. Fold in the bananas.

3   Place half the mixture in a separate bowl; sift over the cocoa powder, add the milk and fold together. Stir the ground ginger into the plain banana mixture. Place alternate spoonfuls of each mixture into the bread pan, then gently swirl a sharp knife or skewer through the mixture to create a marbled effect.

4   Place the bread pan in position in the machine and close the lid. Set the machine to "Bake Only" for 55 minutes. Press Start.

5   After baking, a fine skewer inserted in the centre of the teabread should come out clean. If the teabread requires further baking, bake on the same setting for a further 5–10 minutes, or until cooked.

6   Remove the bread pan from the machine and leave to stand for 10 minutes, then turn the teabread out onto a wire rack to cool. Dust with icing sugar and cocoa powder, if desired, and serve warm or cold.

apricot & walnut teabread

PREPARATION TIME 20 MINUTES   **COOKING TIME** 1–1¼ HOURS   **MAKES** 1 LOAF (SERVES 10)

280g (10oz / 2 cups) plain white flour
2½ tsp baking powder
1½ tsp ground mixed spice
85g (3oz) butter, diced
85g (3oz / ½ cup packed) soft light brown sugar

200g (7oz / 1¼ cups) ready-to-eat dried apricots, chopped
115g (4oz / ⅔ cup) sultanas
85g (3oz / ⅔ cup) walnuts, chopped
200ml (7fl oz / ¾ cup) milk
1 egg, beaten

1   Remove the kneading blade from the bread pan. Remove the bread pan from the machine, grease and line the base and sides of the pan and set aside.

2   Sift the flour, baking powder and mixed spice into a bowl, then lightly rub in the butter. Stir in the sugar, apricots, sultanas and walnuts. Gradually beat in the milk and egg until well mixed. Spoon the mixture into the bread pan and level the surface.

3   Place the bread pan in position in the machine and close the lid. Set the machine to "Bake Only" for 60 minutes. Press Start.

4   After baking, a fine skewer inserted in the centre of the teabread should come out clean. If the teabread requires further baking, bake on the same setting for a further 10–15 minutes, or until cooked.

5   Remove the bread pan from the machine using oven gloves, then leave to stand for 5 minutes, before turning the teabread out onto a wire rack to cool. Serve warm or cold in slices.

Variations Use raisins or dried blueberries in place of sultanas. Use hazelnuts or pecans in place of walnuts.

hawaiian fruit teabread

PREPARATION TIME 15 MINUTES, PLUS OVERNIGHT SOAKING   **COOKING TIME** 1–1¼ HOURS

MAKES 1 LOAF (SERVES 10)

225g (8oz / 1¼ cups) mixed ready-to-eat
   dried tropical fruit, chopped
175ml (6fl oz / ⅔ cup) strong hot tea, strained
225g (8oz / 1⅔ cups) plain wholemeal flour
1 tbsp baking powder
1½ tsp ground mixed spice

175g (6oz / scant 1 cup packed) soft light brown sugar
finely grated zest of 1 orange
25g (1oz / ¼ cup) desiccated coconut
1 egg, beaten
4 tbsp milk
sifted icing sugar, to decorate

1 Put the mixed fruit in a large bowl, pour over the hot tea, stir to mix, then leave to soak overnight.

2 The next day, remove the kneading blade from the bread pan. Remove the bread pan from the machine, grease and line the base and sides of the pan and set aside.

3 Combine the flour, baking powder, mixed spice, brown sugar, orange zest and coconut in a bowl. Add to the soaked fruits, together with the egg and milk, and mix thoroughly. Spoon into the bread pan and level the surface.

4 Place the bread pan in position in the machine and close the lid. Set the machine to "Bake Only" for 60 minutes. Press Start.

5 After baking, a fine skewer inserted in the centre of the teabread should come out clean. If the loaf requires further baking, bake on the same setting for a further 10–15 minutes, or until cooked.

6 Remove the bread pan from the machine using oven gloves. Leave to stand for 5 minutes, before turning the teabread out onto a wire rack to cool. Dust with sifted icing sugar. Serve warm or cold in slices.

teacakes

PREPARATION TIME 15 MINUTES, PLUS MIXING & KNEADING TIME IN BREADMACHINE, PLUS RISING
COOKING TIME 20–25 MINUTES   **MAKES** 8 TEACAKES

300ml (½ pint / 1¼ cups) milk (at room
    temperature), plus extra for glazing
450g (1lb / 3 cups) strong plain white flour
1¼ tsp salt

25g (1oz / 2 tbsp) caster sugar
25g (1oz) butter, diced
1½ tsp fast-action dried yeast
115g (4oz / ⅔ cup) currants

1   Pour the milk into the bread pan. Sprinkle over the flour, covering the milk completely. Place the salt, sugar and butter in separate corners of the pan. Make a small indent in the centre of the flour and add the yeast. Close the lid, set the machine to "Basic Raisin Dough" (or equivalent), or "Dough", and press Start.

2   Add the currants when the machine makes a sound (beeps) to add extra ingredients during the kneading cycle (or add 5 minutes before the end of the kneading cycle). Meanwhile, grease 2 baking sheets and set aside.

3   When the dough is ready, remove it from the machine, knock it back on a lightly floured surface, then divide the dough into 8 equal portions. Roll and shape each portion of the dough into a round teacake and prick each one twice on top with a fork. Place on the baking sheets, cover and leave to rise in a warm place until doubled in size.

4   Preheat the oven to 200°C/400°F/gas mark 6. Brush the teacakes with a little milk, then bake for 20–25 minutes, or until risen and golden brown. Transfer to a wire rack to cool. To serve, split each teacake in half, toast lightly and spread with butter or jam.

teacake fingers

PREPARATION TIME 15 MINUTES, PLUS MIXING & KNEADING TIME IN BREADMACHINE, PLUS RISING
COOKING TIME 20 MINUTES   **MAKES** 12 TEACAKE FINGERS

150ml (¼ pint / ⅔ cup) milk (at room temperature)
175ml (6fl oz / ⅔ cup) warm water (or according to
   bread-mix packet instructions)
500g (1lb 2oz) packet white bread mix
2 tbsp caster sugar

1 tsp ground mixed spice
25g (1oz) butter, diced
115g (4oz / ⅔ cup) sultanas
55g (2oz / ⅓ cup) chopped mixed peel
beaten egg, for glazing

1 Pour the milk and correct amount of water into the bread pan. Sprinkle over the bread mix, covering the liquid completely. Sprinkle over the sugar and mixed spice, then dot the butter over the surface. Close the lid, set the machine to "Basic Raisin Dough" (or equivalent), or "Dough", and press Start.

2 Add the sultanas and mixed peel when the machine makes a sound (beeps) to add extra ingredients during the kneading cycle (or add 5 minutes before the end of the kneading cycle).

3 Meanwhile, grease or flour 2 baking sheets and set aside. When the dough is ready, remove it from the machine, knock it back on a lightly floured surface, then divide the dough into 12 equal portions.

4 Roll and shape each portion of the dough into a long roll or finger shape and place on the baking sheets. Cover and leave to rise in a warm place for about 30 minutes, or until doubled in size.

5 Preheat the oven to 190°C/375°F/gas mark 5. Brush the teacakes with beaten egg, then bake for about 20 minutes, or until risen and golden brown. Transfer to a wire rack to cool. Serve split, lightly toasted and spread with butter.

english muffins

PREPARATION TIME 20 MINUTES, PLUS MIXING & KNEADING TIME IN BREADMACHINE, PLUS RISING
COOKING TIME 35 MINUTES   **MAKES** 8–10 MUFFINS

140ml (4½fl oz / ½ cup) milk (at room temperature)
125ml (4fl oz / ½ cup) water
55g (2oz) butter, melted
450g (1lb / 3 cups) strong plain white flour

1½ tsp salt
1 tsp caster sugar
1½ tsp fast-action dried yeast
sunflower oil, for greasing

1   Pour the milk and water into a bowl, add the melted butter and whisk well. Pour the mixture into the bread pan. Sprinkle over the flour, covering the liquid completely. Place the salt and sugar in separate corners of the pan. Make a small indent in the centre of the flour and add the yeast. Close the lid, set the machine to "Dough" and press Start.

2   Meanwhile, generously flour a large baking sheet and set aside. When the dough is ready, remove it from the machine, knock it back on a lightly floured surface, then divide the dough into 8–10 equal portions.

3   Shape each portion of the dough into a round with straight sides, each about 1–2 cm (½–¾in) thick. Place on the baking sheet, cover and leave to rise in a warm place for about 30–40 minutes, or until springy to the touch.

4   Brush a griddle or large, heavy-based frying pan with a little oil and heat until warm. Carefully transfer 3–4 muffins onto the griddle and cook over a moderate heat for 8–10 minutes, or until golden brown underneath. Turn them over and cook the other side for about 8 minutes, or until golden brown.

5   Remove the muffins from the pan and wrap them in a clean tea towel, if serving warm. Otherwise, transfer them to a wire rack to cool. Cook the remaining muffins in batches.

6   To serve, split the muffins open and serve with butter. If serving from cold, toast the muffins on both sides, then split and spread with butter.

english wholemeal muffins

PREPARATION TIME 20 MINUTES, PLUS MIXING & KNEADING TIME IN BREADMACHINE, PLUS RISING
COOKING TIME 35 MINUTES   **MAKES** 8–10 MUFFINS

350ml (12fl oz / 1⅓ cups) milk (at room temperature)
225g (8oz / 1½ cups) strong plain white flour
225g (8oz / 1⅔ cups) strong plain wholemeal flour
1½ tsp salt

1 tsp caster sugar
15g (½oz) butter, diced
1½ tsp fast-action dried yeast
sunflower oil, for greasing

1   Pour the milk into the bread pan. Sprinkle over each flour in turn, covering the milk completely. Place the salt, sugar and butter in separate corners of the pan. Make a small indent in the centre of the flour and add the yeast. Close the lid, set the machine to "Dough" and press Start.

2   Meanwhile, generously flour a large baking sheet and set aside. When the dough is ready, remove it from the machine, knock it back on a lightly floured surface, then divide the dough into 8–10 equal portions.

3   Shape each portion of the dough into a round with straight sides, about 1–2cm (½–¾in) thick. Place on the baking sheet, cover and leave to rise in a warm place for about 30 minutes, or until almost doubled in size.

4   Brush a griddle or large, heavy-based frying pan with a little oil and heat until warm. Carefully transfer 3–4 muffins onto the griddle and cook over a moderate heat for 7–10 minutes, or until golden brown underneath. Turn them over and cook the other side for about 7 minutes, or until golden brown.

5   Remove the muffins from the pan and wrap them in a clean tea towel, if serving warm. Otherwise, transfer them to a wire rack to cool. Cook the remaining muffins in batches.

6   To serve, split the muffins open and serve with butter. If serving from cold, toast the muffins on both sides, then split and spread with butter.

CHAPTER 7

gluten-free breads

For those with a sensitivity to gluten, this chapter will be an invaluable source of creative and tasty recipes.

Gluten-free breads, by the very nature of the ingredients used to create them, tend to be slightly different in texture and flavour from ordinary breads, but are just as appealing and delicious. They have a slightly more crumbly, closer, but light texture, and many are enjoyed at their best when served warm and freshly baked.

There is an excellent selection of gluten-free recipes in this chapter, including Basic Gluten-free White Bread and Basic Gluten-free Brown Bread, Fresh Herb Bread and Italian Tomato Bread, as well as tasty sweet recipes such as Spiced Honey Loaf and Apricot & Cranberry Teabread.

basic gluten-free white bread (pictured right)

PREPARATION TIME 10 MINUTES   **COOKING TIME** VARIES ACCORDING TO BREADMACHINE

MAKES 1 LOAF (SERVES 10–12)

325ml (11fl oz / 1⅓ cups) milk (at room temperature)
4 tbsp sunflower oil
2 eggs, lightly beaten
450g (1lb / 3 cups) gluten-free white bread flour

2 tbsp caster sugar
1 tsp salt
1 sachet (7g / ¼oz) fast-action dried yeast

1   Pour the milk into a bowl, add the oil and eggs and whisk together well to mix. Pour the mixture into the bread pan. Sprinkle over the flour, covering the liquid completely. Sprinkle the sugar evenly over the flour, then add the salt. Make a small indent in the centre of the flour and add the yeast.

2   Close the lid, set the machine to "Rapid Bake" (or equivalent), then select the loaf size and crust type. Press Start.

3   A couple of minutes after mixing has begun, lift the lid of the machine briefly and scrape down the sides of the pan with a plastic spatula to ensure even mixing. Close the lid once again.

4   After baking, remove the bread pan from the machine and turn the loaf out onto a wire rack to cool. Serve in slices.

basic gluten-free brown bread

PREPARATION TIME 10 MINUTES   **COOKING TIME** VARIES ACCORDING TO BREADMACHINE

MAKES 1 LOAF (SERVES 10–12)

325ml (11fl oz / 1⅓ cups) milk (at room temperature)
4 tbsp sunflower oil
2 eggs, lightly beaten
450g (1lb / 3 cups) gluten-free brown bread flour

2 tbsp caster sugar
1 tsp salt
1 sachet (7g / ¼oz) fast-action dried yeast

1   Pour the milk into a bowl, add the oil and eggs and whisk together well to mix. Pour the mixture into the bread pan. Sprinkle over the flour, covering the liquid completely. Sprinkle the sugar evenly over the flour, then add the salt. Make a small indent in the centre of the flour and add the yeast.

2   Close the lid, set the machine to "Rapid Bake" (or equivalent), then select the loaf size and crust type. Press Start.

3   A couple of minutes after mixing has begun, lift the lid of the machine briefly and scrape down the sides of the pan with a plastic spatula to ensure even mixing. Close the lid once again.

4   After baking, remove the bread pan from the machine and turn the loaf out onto a wire rack to cool. Serve in slices.

fresh herb bread

PREPARATION TIME 15 MINUTES   **COOKING TIME** VARIES ACCORDING TO BREADMACHINE

MAKES 1 LOAF (SERVES 10–12)

400g (14oz / 2⅔ cups) gluten-free white bread flour
55g (2oz / ½ cup) gram (chickpea) flour
275ml (9½fl oz / 1 cup) water
2 eggs, beaten
4 tbsp olive oil
4 tbsp chopped fresh mixed herbs (such as parsley, basil, oregano and chives)

55g (2oz / ⅓ cup) fresh Parmesan cheese, finely grated
1 tbsp caster sugar
1½ tsp salt
2½ tsp fast-action dried yeast

1   Combine the flours and set aside. Pour the water into a bowl, add the eggs, oil and chopped herbs and whisk together well to mix. Pour the mixture into the bread pan. Sprinkle over the cheese, then sprinkle over the mixed flours, covering the liquid completely. Sprinkle the sugar evenly over the flour, then add the salt. Make a small indent in the centre of the flour and add the yeast.

2   Close the lid, set the machine to "Rapid Bake" (or equivalent), then select the loaf size and crust type. Press Start.

3   A couple of minutes after mixing has begun, lift the lid of the machine briefly and scrape down the sides of the pan with a plastic spatula to ensure even mixing. Close the lid once again.

4   After baking, remove the bread pan from the machine and turn the loaf out onto a wire rack to cool. Serve in slices.

mixed seed loaf

PREPARATION TIME 10 MINUTES   **COOKING TIME** VARIES ACCORDING TO BREADMACHINE

MAKES 1 LOAF (SERVES 10–12)

325ml (11fl oz / 1⅓ cups) milk (at room
   temperature)
4 tbsp sunflower oil
2 eggs, lightly beaten
450g (1lb / 3 cups) gluten-free white bread flour

5 tbsp mixed seeds (such as sunflower, pumpkin,
   caraway, poppy seeds and linseeds)
2 tbsp caster sugar
1 tsp salt
1 sachet (7g / ¼oz) fast-action dried yeast

1   Pour the milk into a bowl, add the oil and eggs and whisk together well to mix. Pour the mixture into the bread pan. Sprinkle over the flour, covering the liquid completely. Sprinkle the mixed seeds evenly over the flour. Sprinkle over the sugar, then add the salt. Make a small indent in the centre of the flour and add the yeast.

2   Close the lid, set the machine to "Rapid Bake" (or equivalent), then select the loaf size and crust type. Press Start.

3   A couple of minutes after mixing has begun, lift the lid of the machine briefly and scrape down the sides of the pan with a plastic spatula to ensure even mixing. Close the lid once again.

4   After baking, remove the bread pan from the machine and turn the loaf out onto a wire rack to cool. Serve in slices.

italian tomato bread

PREPARATION TIME 15 MINUTES   **COOKING TIME** VARIES ACCORDING TO BREADMACHINE

MAKES 1 LOAF (SERVES 10–12)

325ml (11fl oz / 1⅓ cups) milk (at room temperature)
2 tbsp oil from a jar of sun-dried tomatoes
2 tbsp olive oil
2 eggs, lightly beaten
55g (2oz / ⅓ cup) fresh Parmesan cheese,
    finely grated

85g (3oz / ¾ cup) sun-dried tomatoes in oil
    (drained weight), patted dry and chopped
450g (1lb / 3 cups) gluten-free brown bread flour
2 tbsp caster sugar
1 tsp salt
1 sachet (7g / ¼oz) fast-action dried yeast

1   Pour the milk into a bowl, add the oils and eggs and whisk together well to mix. Pour the mixture into
the bread pan. Sprinkle the cheese over the milk mixture, followed by the tomatoes. Sprinkle over the
flour, covering the liquid, cheese and tomatoes completely. Sprinkle the sugar evenly over the flour,
then add the salt. Make a small indent in the centre of the flour and add the yeast.

2   Close the lid, set the machine to "Rapid Bake" (or equivalent), then select the loaf size and crust type.
Press Start.

3   A couple of minutes after mixing has begun, lift the lid of the machine briefly and scrape down the
sides of the pan with a plastic spatula to ensure even mixing. Close the lid once again.

4   After baking, remove the bread pan from the machine and turn the loaf out onto a wire rack to cool.
Serve in slices.

cheese & mustard bread

PREPARATION TIME 15 MINUTES   **COOKING TIME** VARIES ACCORDING TO BREADMACHINE

MAKES 1 LOAF (SERVES 10–12)

400g (14oz / 2⅔ cups) gluten-free white bread flour
55g (2oz / ½ cup) gram (chickpea) flour
300ml (½ pint / 1¼ cups) water
2 eggs, beaten
4 tbsp olive oil
3 tbsp gluten-free wholegrain mustard

85g (3oz / ⅔ cup) mature Cheddar cheese,
    finely grated
1 tbsp caster sugar
1½ tsp salt
2½ tsp fast-action dried yeast

1   Combine the flours and set aside. Place the water in a bowl, add the eggs, oil and mustard and whisk together well to mix. Pour the mixture into the bread pan. Sprinkle over the cheese, then sprinkle over the flours, covering the liquid and cheese completely. Sprinkle the sugar evenly over the flour, then add the salt. Make a small indent in the centre of the flour and add the yeast.

2   Close the lid, set the machine to "Rapid Bake" (or equivalent), then select the loaf size and crust type. Press Start.

3   A couple of minutes after mixing has begun, lift the lid of the machine briefly and scrape down the sides of the pan with a plastic spatula to ensure even mixing. Close the lid once again.

4   After baking, remove the bread pan from the machine and turn the loaf out onto a wire rack to cool. Serve in slices.

herbed olive bread

PREPARATION TIME 15 MINUTES   **COOKING TIME** VARIES ACCORDING TO BREADMACHINE

MAKES 1 LOAF (SERVES 10–12)

325ml (11fl oz / 1⅓ cups) milk (at room temperature)
4 tbsp olive oil
2 eggs, lightly beaten
2 tsp dried Italian herb seasoning
85g (3oz / ½ cup) fresh Parmesan cheese,
    finely grated

85g (3oz / ½ cup) pitted black olives (drained
    weight), chopped
450g (1lb / 3 cups) gluten-free brown bread flour
2 tbsp caster sugar
1 tsp salt
1 sachet (7g / ¼oz) fast-action dried yeast

1   Pour the milk into a bowl, add the oil, eggs and dried herbs and whisk together well to mix. Pour the
    mixture into the bread pan. Sprinkle the cheese over the milk, followed by the olives. Sprinkle over
    the flour, covering the liquid, cheese and olives completely. Sprinkle the sugar evenly over the flour,
    then add the salt. Make a small indent in the centre of the flour and add the yeast.

2   Close the lid, set the machine to "Rapid Bake" (or equivalent), then select the loaf size and crust type.
    Press Start.

3   A couple of minutes after mixing has begun, lift the lid of the machine briefly and scrape down the
    sides of the pan with a plastic spatula to ensure even mixing. Close the lid once again.

4   After baking, remove the bread pan from the machine and turn the loaf out onto a wire rack to cool.
    Serve in slices.

spiced honey loaf

PREPARATION TIME 20 MINUTES   **COOKING TIME** 50–60 MINUTES   **MAKES** 1 LOAF (SERVES 8)

115g (4oz / ⅔ cup packed) soft light brown sugar
85g (3oz) butter
175g (6oz / ½ cup) thick (set) honey
225g (8oz / 1½ cups) gluten-free plain white flour
a pinch of salt

1 tsp gluten-free baking powder
2 tsp ground mixed spice
1 egg, beaten
150ml (¼ pint / ⅔ cup) milk

1 Remove the kneading blade from the bread pan. Remove the bread pan from the machine, grease and line the base and sides of the pan and set aside.

2 Place the sugar, butter and honey in a saucepan and heat gently until melted, stirring. Remove the pan from the heat and cool slightly. Sift the flour, salt, baking powder and mixed spice into a bowl and make a well in the centre. Mix together the egg and milk and pour into the centre of the dry ingredients together with the melted honey mixture. Beat together using a wooden spoon until smooth and thoroughly mixed. Pour the mixture into the bread pan.

3 Place the bread pan in position in the machine and close the lid. Set the machine to "Bake Only" for 50 minutes. Press Start.

4 After baking, a fine skewer inserted in the centre of the loaf should come out clean. If the loaf requires further baking, bake on the same setting for a further 5–10 minutes, or until cooked.

5 Remove the bread pan from the machine using oven gloves, then leave to stand for 5 minutes, before turning the loaf out onto a wire rack to cool. Serve warm or cold in slices.

Variations Use golden syrup in place of honey. Use ground ginger or cinnamon in place of mixed spice.

sticky spiced teabread

PREPARATION TIME 20 MINUTES, PLUS COOLING   **COOKING TIME** 50–60 MINUTES   **MAKES** 1 LOAF (SERVES 8)

115g (4oz / ⅔ cup packed) soft light brown sugar
85g (3oz) butter
115g (4oz / ⅓ cup) golden syrup
55g (2oz / ¼ cup) black treacle
225g (8oz / 1½ cups) gluten-free plain white flour
a pinch of salt

1 tsp gluten-free baking powder
2 tsp ground mixed spice
1 tsp ground ginger
1 egg, beaten
150ml (¼ pint / ⅔ cup) milk

1   Remove the kneading blade from the bread pan. Remove the bread pan from the machine, grease and
    line the base and sides of the pan and set aside.

2   Place the sugar, butter, syrup and black treacle in a saucepan and heat gently until melted, stirring.
    Remove the pan from the heat and cool slightly. Sift the flour, salt, baking powder and ground spices
    into a bowl and make a well in the centre. Mix together the egg and milk and pour into the centre of
    the dry ingredients together with the melted syrup mixture. Beat together using a wooden spoon until
    smooth and thoroughly mixed. Pour the mixture into the bread pan.

3   Place the bread pan in position in the machine and close the lid. Set the machine to "Bake Only" for
    50 minutes. Press Start.

4   After baking, a fine skewer inserted in the centre of the tealoaf should come out clean. If the tealoaf
    requires further baking, bake on the same setting for a further 5–10 minutes, or until cooked.

5   Remove the bread pan from the machine using oven gloves, then leave to stand for 5 minutes, before
    turning the tealoaf out onto a wire rack to cool. Serve warm or cold in slices.

Variation Use ground cinnamon in place of ginger.

apricot & cranberry teabread

PREPARATION TIME 20 MINUTES   **COOKING TIME** 1–1¼ HOURS   **MAKES** 1 LOAF (SERVES 10)

225g (8oz / 1½ cups) gluten-free plain white flour
2 tsp gluten-free baking powder
115g (4oz) butter, diced
115g (4oz / ⅔ cup packed) soft light brown sugar
finely grated zest of 1 small orange

175g (6oz / 1 cup) ready-to-eat dried apricots, chopped
175g (6oz / 1 cup) sweetened dried cranberries
2 eggs, beaten
150ml (¼ pint / ⅔ cup) milk

1   Remove the kneading blade from the bread pan. Remove the bread pan from the machine, grease and line the base and sides of the pan and set aside.

2   Sift the flour and baking powder into a bowl, then lightly rub in the butter. Stir in the sugar, orange zest and dried fruit. Add the eggs and milk and mix together until thoroughly combined. Spoon the mixture into the bread pan and level the surface.

3   Place the bread pan in position in the machine and close the lid. Set the machine to "Bake Only" for 60 minutes. Press Start.

4   After baking, a fine skewer inserted in the centre of the teabread should come out clean. If the teabread requires further baking, bake on the same setting for a further 10–15 minutes, or until cooked.

5   Remove the bread pan from the machine using oven gloves, then leave to stand for 5 minutes, before turning the teabread out onto a wire rack to cool. Serve warm or cold in slices.

Acknowledgements

My special thanks go to my husband, Robbie, for his continued support
and encouragement with this book and for his tireless tasting of many of
the recipes. My sincere thanks also go to Sarah Bradford and Bev Saunder
for all their dedicated hard work testing recipes, and to Gwen Whiting for
her help with typing recipes.